'Involved' fathering and child well-being

Fathers' involvement with secondary school age children

Elaine Welsh, Ann Buchanan, Eirini Flouri, Jane Lewis

GW00673415

JR
1904
2004
JOSEPH
ROWNTREE
FOUNDATION

national
children's
bureau
making a difference

Joseph Rowntree Foundation

The Joseph Rowntree Foundation has supported this project as part of its programme of research and innovative development projects, which it hopes will be of value to policy makers, practitioners and service users.

National Children's Bureau

NCB promotes the voices, interests and well-being of all children and young people across every aspect of their lives.

NCB aims to:
■ challenge disadvantage in childhood
■ work with children and young people to ensure they are involved in all matters that affect their lives
■ promote multidisciplinary cross-agency partnerships and good practice
■ influence government through policy development and advocacy
■ undertake high quality research and work from an evidence-based perspective
■ disseminate information to all those working with children and young people, and to children and young people themselves

The views expressed in this book are those of the authors and not necessarily those of the National Children's Bureau, the Joseph Rowntree Foundation or the University of Oxford.

Published by the National Children's Bureau for the Joseph Rowntree Foundation

National Children's Bureau, 8 Wakley Street, London EC1V 7QE
Tel: 020 7843 6000. Website: www.ncb.org.uk
Registered Charity number 258825

Contents

Preface

This research was conceived as both quantitative and qualitative and as an interdisciplinary endeavour. Ann Buchanan and Eirini Flouri (both psychologists) took responsibility for the quantitative study and Elaine Welsh (a sociologist) and Jane Lewis (a social policy analyst) were responsible for the qualitative element of the study. We would all like to record our thanks to Caroline Lee and Sophie Sarre, who played a major part in the interviewing, as well as Vincci Lau who helped input survey data.

We would also like to thank members of the Advisory Board (Adrienne Burgess, Lynda Clarke, John Eekelaar, Eunice Halliday, Charlie Lewis, Bren Neale, Yvonne Neary, Tony Newman, Martin Richards and Susan Taylor) for their helpful and constructive comments throughout this research project as well as the Joseph Rowntree Foundation for funding the research.

The research would not have taken place without the assistance of staff in the three schools and the young people and their parents who shared their expertise with us. We are very grateful to them for taking the time to complete the questionnaires and to be interviewed. To all of them, we would like to say a special thank you.

The authors would like to acknowledge the skilful assistance of Jenny Reynolds in editing the report and making it more accessible. We are very grateful for her help.

Executive summary

This large-scale study explored the nature of fathering and its impact on children in Britain in the twenty-first century. More than 2,000 teenagers from three schools (inner city, suburban and rural) and their parents took part in a survey using standardised measures of father involvement and well-being and 26 co-resident parents and their children were interviewed in their homes. Because of problems in obtaining responses from non-resident fathers and from all three members of the family, sub-samples of respondents were used for different aspects of the analysis. This dependence on 'select' groups may have affected the findings.

Involvement

The survey found that:

- Overall, resident dads were rated as more involved by their children than non-resident dads. However, the ratings of non-resident fathers' involvement varied widely and some non-resident fathers were rated more highly than resident dads.

- Ratings also varied by the level of conflict between parents and a family's financial situation. Children rated father involvement lower in high conflict families and in families where children received free school meals.

- Although non-resident dads were rated as less involved, 5 per cent of the 11 per cent of children in step-families considered their biological father to be their main father figure.

The interviews:

- Echoed the findings of other research and revealed a fairly traditional view of fathering, with fathers more involved in the 'macro' or overseeing aspects of their children's lives rather than the mundane details of day-to-day living.

Families described dads' responsibilities as 'being there', providing for the family, planning and guiding. Relatively few fathers took responsibility for their children's everyday lives.

■ Most fathers were emotionally close to their children, and knew the type of things their children liked to do, although they were not involved in regular activities with them.

■ Many fathers claimed that fathering just came 'naturally' but some admitted they lacked the confidence or the necessary skills to form close relationships with their children. In some cases, communication was constrained because dad used a 'jokey' style of relating.

Links between fathers' involvement and children's well-being

The survey indicated that:

■ Children with resident fathers were slightly better adjusted than children in separated families.

■ Children in families with a resident father were better adjusted if they were living with their biological father, their father had good mental health and he was well educated and highly involved.

■ Children were more likely to be experiencing emotional and behavioural problems if there was conflict between the parents.

■ Fathers perceived sons to be more difficult than daughters.

The analysis of separated families showed that:

■ Children were more likely to be experiencing emotional and behavioural problems if there was a high level of conflict between the resident and non-resident parent and if the mother was not very involved.

■ The analysis also revealed an unexpected finding. Whereas a resident mother's involvement was significantly associated with greater child well-being, father involvement was not. However, caution needs to be exercised in interpreting this finding. It is possible that it reflects the study's recruitment process and potential biases in the sample.

Factors affecting fathers' involvement

The survey found that:

- Resident dads were more likely to be involved with their children if the mother was involved, if the father held egalitarian gender role attitudes and if the children were well adjusted. The more difficult fathers believed their children to be, the less likely fathers were to be involved.

- The survey identified families on a continuum of parental involvement and family well-being. At one end of the spectrum are more 'child-centred families' where the parents are highly involved, hold egalitarian attitudes, have high levels of self-esteem and are part of a supportive and amicable relationship.

- At the other end of the continuum are more 'adult-centred' families with increasingly uninvolved parents with few emotional and social resources at their disposal. At the extreme, these are characterised by relatively uninvolved parents who argue frequently and have inequitable gender attitudes. Moreover, dad is likely to be poorly educated and mum, dad and children are likely to be suffering from low self-esteem or mental health difficulties.

The interviews pointed to the difficulties dads faced in getting involved with their teenage children.

- Young people who found the transition to adulthood more difficult than their peers often also had an uninvolved father.

- Uninvolved dads were also often in conflict with their partner and so seemed to lack the supportive relationship that the interviews showed boosted dads' confidence in and knowledge of how to get involved.

What affects non-resident dads' involvement?

The survey revealed that:

- Levels of contact in the sample were higher than those reported by other studies.

- Non-resident dads were more likely to be involved when the mum was highly involved and if the parents had separated recently. Conflict between the parents mitigated against dads' involvement.

- The insight into resident fathers' involvement permitted by the interviews points to the obstacles non-resident dads face in being a part of their children's lives. Because a large part of the 'being there' role is not available to them, non-resident dads have to establish new roles and relationships if their contact is to be rewarding and effective.

Policy dilemmas

The researchers conclude that the findings point to the value of holistic intervention. Promoting better father–child relationships is about enhancing whole family well-being. Targeting one problem or one family relationship is not enough. Potential avenues for intervention include:

- helping parents to build mutually supportive relationships and to reduce conflict both before and after separation;
- measures to improve children's mental health;
- helping parents to understand the impact of their behaviour and their relationship on each others' parenting;
- helping dads to develop confidence in their parenting and communication skills.

1. Background

Introduction

The rapid social change of the last three decades has created upheaval in family life. Important influences include: the increase in the numbers of mothers working outside of the home; the gender equality movement; a steep rise in divorce rates and subsequent increase in second families; and the increase in the number of children born outside of marriage (e.g. see Lewis, 2000). These changes have created a shift in the way 'parents parent' and, in particular, expectations about fathers' involvement in family life.

While there has been a considerable amount of research into fatherhood (e.g. see Lewis, 2000 for a review), there remain a number of gaps and inconsistencies in our knowledge. As Lewis concluded 'there is widespread confusion and disagreement over the contribution men make to contemporary family life'. This research explores some of the confusion by examining the following questions about fatherhood in both intact and separated families:

- What does it mean to be an involved father?

- What factors influence fathers' involvement?

- Does being an involved father benefit the children?

What does being an involved father mean?

There already exists a significant body of research into fathers' involvement with their children (e.g. see Lamb, 1986; Hawkins and others, 2002). Initially, research measured father involvement in terms of the time fathers spent on different activities. Subsequently, researchers have developed measures of the type of activities in which fathers were involved and which promoted the development of their children (Pleck, 1997). This study unites these aspects of father involvement by considering both the level of father involvement in contemporary family life as well as the relationship between dads' involvement and children's well-being.

What factors influence fathers' involvement?

A well-supported model, and one that underpins this research, has identified five components of fathering (Doherty, Kouneski and Erickson, 1998). The model, outlined in Figure 1.1, includes: (i) contextual factors, such as employment and social support, (ii) father factors, such as knowledge, well-being, and commitment, (iii) mother factors, such as the mother's attitude towards and expectations of the father, (iv) co-parental relationships, such as levels of commitment, cooperation, and conflict, (v) child factors, including temperament, age and behaviour.

Are the factors that influence involvement the same for fathers who live with their children compared with dads who live elsewhere? Drawing on different family members' perspectives, the research re-examines findings that have suggested that non-resident fathers' involvement is affected by the quality of the father's ongoing relationship with the mother (Amato and Rezac, 1994), and the characteristics of the child (Hetherington and Stanley-Hagan, 1997).

Figure 1.1 Factors influencing father involvement (reproduced by kind permission of William Doherty)

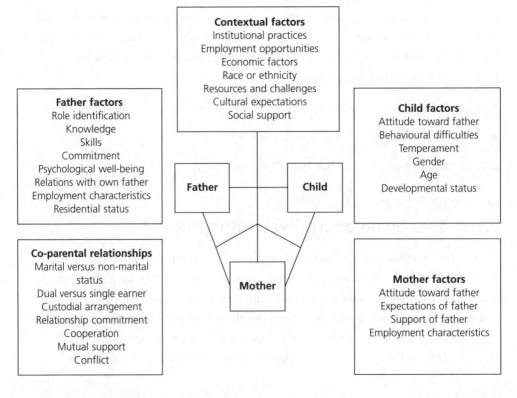

How does a father's involvement affect his child?

Current family policy is underpinned by the belief that children benefit from their fathers' involvement in both intact and separated families. Concerns about fathers' lack of involvement following divorce have led to moves to encourage contact. For example, the Lord Chancellor's Department's commitment to encouraging contact is exemplified in its report to the Lord Chancellor *Making Contact Work* (2002). But does the research support this policy? Research suggests that father involvement is beneficial for children's well-being and achievement, particularly adolescents, in intact families (Lamb, 1997; Marsiglio and others, 2000; Harris, Furstenberg and Marmer, 1998). But the research is more ambiguous about the benefits of involvement after separation. While research has identified links between the payment of child support and children's well-being the evidence concerning the benefit of father care is more complex and in some cases less convincing (e.g. Crockett, Eggebeen and Hawkins, 1993; King, 1994). A number of studies have found no relationship between frequency of contact and children's adjustment. However, a meta-analysis concluded that father contact was beneficial, although this depended on the degree of conflict between the parents, the nature of the dad's involvement, mother's acceptance, and regular payment of child support (Amato and Gilbreth, 1999).

Fathers' involvement in separated families has to be understood in the context of the impact of the divorce on the children. Although most children adjust normally to their parents' divorce given time, important influences on their adjustment include: school achievement, conduct, psychological adjustment, self-concept and social adjustment, and the children's relationship with his or her parents (Amato and Keith, 1991). This research attempts to control for the impact of some of these factors.

How children fare is particularly affected by the level and nature of conflict in the relationship between the parents (Rodgers and Pryor, 1998). Conflict can have a damaging impact both while parents are together and following divorce (Hetherington and Stanley-Hagen, 1999; Grych and Fincham, 1999). Conflict also affects parenting although it is more disruptive to fathering than mothering (Coiro and Emery, 1998; Lewis, Maka and Papacosta, 1997). A question that remains unanswered is whether the detrimental impact of parental conflict outweighs the potential benefits of a father's continuing involvement. While the current study cannot fully answer this question it adds to the body of knowledge around it.

Outline of the research and the report

Aims and objectives

This study aims to contribute to the debate surrounding the nature and benefits of resident and non-resident dads' involvement by examining the following questions:

- What does father involvement mean to mums, dads and their children?

- How involved are resident and non-resident fathers with their children?

- What factors promote or hinder fathers' involvement?

- How does a father's involvement affect his child's well-being – whether he lives with the child or resides elsewhere?

Study outline

While previous research has addressed some of these questions, this study examines dads' involvement from the different perspectives of each family member. The research involved a large-scale survey of children and their parents and follow-up interviews with a small number of these families. Details of the research methodology are outlined in Chapter Two. Chapter Three explores intact families' accounts of what being an involved father means. Chapter Four reports on young people's ratings of their resident and non-resident fathers. The links between fathers' involvement and their children's well-being are explored in Chapter Five while Chapters Six and Seven explore the factors that influence dads' involvement in intact and separated families respectively. Policy dilemmas are discussed in Chapter Eight.

2. The study

The study involved three stages of fieldwork. These covered:

- a web consultation with young people;
- a survey of young people and their parents drawn from three local schools;
- in-depth interviews with a small sub-sample of the young people who took part in the survey and their parents.

Figure 2.1 summarises the study design. Further details about the number of survey returns and the methodology are given in the appendices.

Figure 2.1 The research design

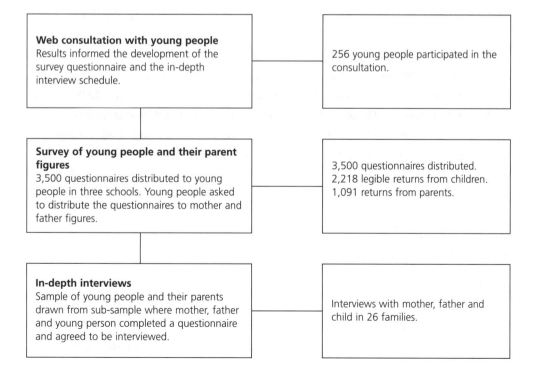

The web consultation

A total of 256 young people participated in a web consultation about their fathers. The findings (not reported here) were used to identify issues to be covered in the survey and in-depth interviews.

The survey

The survey involved young people in an inner city, suburban and rural secondary school. The three schools were all within the average range of Ofsted ratings.

The survey recruitment process

The young people completed the questionnaires in class. They were then invited to take home two identical questionnaires: one to give to the person they felt to be their mother and the other to the person they felt to be their father. Appendix A summarises the recruitment process and the number of questionnaires returned.

Six hundred of the young people's questionnaires were either illegible or incomplete. Hand analysis revealed that most of these questionnaires were from younger children and it is possible that the questions were too difficult for their reading abilities. As a result, older adolescents are over represented in the survey. In two schools the survey took place soon after the attack on the World Trade Center in New York on 11 September, 2001. Some of the unused questionnaires were covered with disturbed comments and drawings. Overall, data were used from 2,218 children and 1,091 parents (although four parents did not state their gender and so are excluded from any mother/father analysis); 312 of the parents were couples. In the case of 265 families there were data from all three family members, but in only 233 of these families were all three members living together, and only 203 of these families comprised both biological parents.

Measures used in the survey

The scales and measures used in the questionnaire covered different aspects of family life and well-being. Details are contained in Appendix B. The two scales central to the study are the Inventory of Parental Involvement, of Hawkins and others (2002) and Goodman's (1997) Strengths and Difficulties Questionnaire.

Inventory of Father Involvement, Hawkins and others (2002)

Involvement was measured using the Inventory of Father Involvement (see Appendix C for details). It comprises a 26-item, 5-point scale with a maximum score of 130. The scale is a continuum and as such there is no cut off point representing an 'involved' or 'uninvolved' dad. The scale was developed for use with fathers from a range of backgrounds and is relevant to fathers in married, unmarried or divorced households. The language of the scale was adapted to suit British respondents.

The scale was completed by children and both parents separately. Children answered the questions thinking about 'the person they thought of as their dad and their mum', which meant that answers could describe either a biological or a social parent. Respondents were asked to rate how well their father did on different aspects of parenting, such as disciplining children or helping them with their homework. In total, the Inventory examines nine dimensions of fathering. Mothers also reported on their own involvement using a similar schedule.

The Goodman Strengths and Difficulties Questionnaire

Children's well-being was assessed using Goodman's (1997) Strengths and Difficulties Questionnaire (SDQ). Parents and children completed different versions of the questionnaire. For example, the young people were asked to respond to a series of statements such as 'I am often unhappy, downhearted or tearful' and 'I am restless, I cannot stay still for long'.

Profile of the children and parents who took part in the survey

The sample reflected those of other national samples. For example, between 13–16 per cent of children in the study received free school meals (depending on whether reported by mothers or children) compared to 12 per cent of children in England (www.qca.org.uk). In 2000, 75 per cent of children in the country lived in two-parent households (Office of National Statistics (ONS), 2000) compared to 66–86 per cent in this sample (the range reflects the difference between mothers' and children's reports). The parental education levels claimed are slightly higher than the national average. Twenty per cent of mothers and 22 per cent of fathers in our sample had a university degree compared with a UK average of 16 per cent (ONS, Social Trends no. 33).

As can be seen from Table 2.1, because fewer parents than children completed a questionnaire there were differences between the parent and children samples.

In particular the children's sample showed higher levels of disadvantage (measured by receipt of free schools meals[1]) and a smaller proportion living in intact families. Therefore, the parent sample is somewhat skewed towards less disadvantaged families. A particular feature of the study was the relatively high percentage of children and parents from minority ethnic groups. This reflected the population of the inner city and suburban schools.

Table 2.1 Details of the mothers, fathers and children who took part in the survey

	Mothers (n=635)*	Fathers (n=452)	Children (n=2218)
Number of:			
Boys			1212**
Girls			989
Mean age	41.3 (SD 6)	44.5 (SD 7.2)	13.5 (SD 1.6)
School location:			
Inner city	23%	23%	28%
Suburban	41%	40%	42%
Rural	36%	37%	30%
Average working hours (employed parents)	24.3 (SD 12.8)	39.6 (SD 14.1)	–
Parents working:			
Full-time	37%	84%	–
Part-time	43%	6%	
Not working	20%	10%	
Proportion of parents with a university degree	20%	23%	20%
Free school meals	13%	7%	16%
House owner/occupier	69%	76%	67%
Ethnic origin:			
White British	78%	76%	62%
Indian+	7%	9%	12%
Other^	15%	15%	26%
Proportion of parents living with:			
Other parent	73%	86%	–
Another partner	5%	6%	
Alone	22%	8%	
Proportion of children living with:			
Both biological parents	–	–	66%
Biological mother and social father			11%
Biological mother			18%
Father alone			2%
Other			3%
Proportion who agreed to a follow-up interview	41%	41%	–

* Questionnaires were received from a total of 1,091 parents, but four parents did not state their gender.
** 17 children did not state their gender.
+ 'Indian' was our second largest single ethnic group.
^ This figure is made up of very small proportions in many different ethnic groups.

[1] Whilst we recognise the limited nature of using free school meals as a measure of poverty, our experience suggests that it is a more reliable way of estimating poverty than asking the children to give parental earnings.

The survey analysis

The number of respondents included in different aspects of the analysis

It was impossible to use the full sample to conduct the analysis because of difficulties in obtaining responses from non-resident fathers and because we obtained responses from both parents and child for a relatively small proportion of the sample. Instead, sub-samples of respondents, summarised in Table 2.2, were created for different elements of the analysis.

Table 2.2 Numbers of respondents used in different phases of the research

Research question	Sample groups used for different elements of the analyses
How involved are resident and non-resident dads? (Chapter Four)	2218 responses from children who took part in the survey.
How well are children with resident dads doing, according to the SDQ measure? (Chapter Five)	409 responses from resident fathers.
How well are children with non-residents dads doing, according to the SDQ measure? (Chapter Five)	520 responses from young people with non-resident dads.
What factors explain resident fathers' involvement? (Chapter Six)	Responses from 233 families where child, mother and father all completed a questionnaire and were resident in the same house (we refer to this as the family sample) and data from the in-depth interviews with 26 families.
What factors explain non-resident fathers' involvement? (Chapter Seven)	520 responses from young people with non-resident dads.

Potential sources of bias

Any survey of this kind and this scale is vulnerable to various sources of bias. The low response rate from parents was a particular concern for this project, but in addition the following issues should be borne in mind.

(i)   The survey relied on children getting their parents to complete the questionnaire. A possible concern, therefore, is that more involved fathers were more likely to complete a questionnaire at their child's request. Indeed, children whose fathers returned a questionnaire rated them slightly higher (rating=107) than children whose fathers did not complete a questionnaire (rating=104), but the difference was not statistically significant (p>0.05).

(ii) Only 34 non-resident fathers returned a questionnaire so children's reports and ratings of their non-resident fathers were used instead of father reports. However, this raises questions about the data. Children who completed a questionnaire about their non-resident father (and we do not know how many refused to complete one) are likely to think more highly of and have more involvement with their non-resident dad than those who did not. This is partly because surveys are vulnerable to 'social desirability' bias – whereby people present themselves and their loved ones in the best light. So children who did not think highly of their dads are unlikely to have completed a questionnaire, although it was not possible to test this. Moreover, the rates of contact with non-resident dads in the sample are higher than in other studies, which suggests the children have more involvement with their fathers compared with other separated families.

(iii) Six hundred children questionnaires were either not completed or illegible. The majority of these were for younger children and reading ability might explain why they were not completed. However, it may also be due to the content of the survey. For example, did these children have particularly difficult relationships with their fathers, which made them reluctant to complete a questionnaire on the subject? It is not possible to test this.

(iv) Out of a possible 3,500 individuals where each respondent could have completed a questionnaire, data for mother, father and child were obtained from only 265 families. We do not know whether these families are significantly different from those where we did not obtain a questionnaire from all members. For example, families with incomplete data may have less involved fathers or may be more prone to conflict, poorer, or differ in other unknown ways.

The in-depth interviews with family members

The interviews provided the opportunity to explore in more depth the meaning of involvement between fathers, mothers and children. Interviews were conducted with 78 individuals in 26 families, selected from a sub-sample of intact, biological families where both parents had indicated that they were willing to be interviewed when they completed the survey questionnaire. Parents who gave their permission to be interviewed were then asked to invite their child to participate. Details of the recruitment process are outlined in Appendix D. The interviews lasted around 90 minutes and were conducted simultaneously with each family member separately. All names have been changed to protect the anonymity of respondents.

Figure 2.2 The interview sample

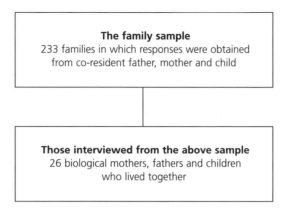

The family sample
233 families in which responses were obtained
from co-resident father, mother and child

Those interviewed from the above sample
26 biological mothers, fathers and children
who lived together

A comparison of the interview sample with the sample of 265[2] children and parents who completed a questionnaire shows that the samples were broadly similar (see Appendix D, Table D.1). The vast majority of those who agreed to be interviewed were in intact families (n=77). Among those who were living apart, and both parents had agreed to be interviewed, there were many different 'family types' (father living with new partner and children to that partner, but not with the child of the 'family group' in our study; father living with new partner but no children to that partner and not living with the child in our study). It was decided to focus on intact families because in other cases there were only one or two examples of each family type, which made it difficult to draw any conclusions about them.

---

[2] 'Family sample' is the label we have given to the 233 families in which father, mother and child responses were available and they all lived together.

3. What does being an involved father mean? Reports from the qualitative interviews

What do fathers do?

This chapter reports on separate interviews with mother, father and child in 26 families. The interviews followed a topic guide that covered questions: about family life; the relationship between the parents; expectations about the roles and responsibilities of dads; and how well dads know their children and get involved in what they do. The research identified four key aspects of fathering:

- macro responsibility;
- micro responsibility;
- activities;
- cognitive and emotional involvement.

Sample source
Reports based on in-depth interviews with mother, father and child in 26 families. The families were drawn from the 77 intact families where all members completed a questionnaire and agreed to a follow-up interview.

Some of these reiterate findings of previous work (e.g. see Warin and others, 1999; Lewis, 2000; Frosh, Phoenix and Pattman, 2002; Hatten, Vinter and Williams, 2002). Similarities and differences with previous research are briefly discussed in each section and in more detail in Chapter Seven. Where exchanges with the interviewer are reported in the text, 'I' denotes interviewer and 'R' the respondent.

Macro responsibility

Macro responsibility captures the way in which fathers are both slightly removed from the daily grind of family life and yet important to it. Three aspects of macro responsibility emerged in the interviews: 'being there'; providing; and guiding.

'Being there'

A recurring theme in the interviews, and one that echoes the findings of previous research (e.g. see Warin and others, 1999; Lupton and Barclay, 1997; Hatten, Vinter and Williams, 2002) was the belief of interviewees that a dad's role was about being available, or just 'being there'. For all members of the family, 'being there' meant being available in both a practical and emotional sense and it also created a feeling of security and stability for the family. Box 3.1 illustrates the different ways respondents talked about 'being there'.

Box 3.1 Typical ideas on 'being there'

Young people
I think I would say a dad is for looking after the children, making sure they are well, basically being there for them.
(Son, family 25)

Being there when you need him. That is about it, being there when you need him.
(Daughter, family 26)

Fathers
I think it's important to be there for them, you know.
(Family 17)

I think the most important job of a parent is emotional being there.
(Family 21)

Mothers
...to me when dad is around then life is safe.
(Family 2)

If the child want their support they've got to be there, be available all the time, they can't just shrug it off and say no...It's no good having loads of money and just giving it to the kids, you've got to physically be there when the children want you.
(Family 9)

For many fathers, 'being there' was a form of passive care that meant being around the children but not necessarily joining in activities or planning aspects of their daily life. This contrasts with the findings of other researchers, listed earlier, where being there was less passive.

Respondents also believed that fathers provided an important balance in family life. For example, responding to questions about why fathers are needed, the daughter from family 11 said:

...you need a dad because you need that side of – you know if you have a mum you have to have a dad to go with it, otherwise the balance is wrong.

Dads offered a different perspective from mothers:

...a father is a steadying influence and he has that influence on a son as well as a daughter and they can see different aspects of things that perhaps a mother wouldn't see.
(Mother, family 11)

Interviewees also believed that fathers protected the family and prevented the children from going astray:

What became obvious to me, particularly being in this area, is that there are so many single mums round here where the father is not present in the household that it has to be a major source of why particularly young boys go astray...they need balance, they need a father figure.
(Father, family 21)

Provider dads

Macro responsibility also involves providing for the family. Fathers believed that providing was a 'taken for granted' function that was qualitatively different from any other fathering activities. Fathers also aspired to provide a certain standard of living for the family. For example, 'providing' was an important part of Dad's identity in family 16:

I: Can you tell me what you think your most important job is as a dad?
R: The safety of my family, providing, we've got a stable home for my wife and them...food on the table, maintaining the house, a nice house to live in.

But providing had to be balanced against a desire to spend a significant amount of time at home. Although a number of respondents had worked hard to provide for their family when their children were young, they also felt that now, having reached the minimum material standard they had set for themselves they would not be prepared to sacrifice more family time for more money. While few of these fathers were the sole breadwinner, they saw providing as a crucial component of fathering regardless of their partner's working status.

Guiding dads

> I provide some sort of beacon for guidance really.
> *(Father, family 21)*

Fathers believed that guiding the social and moral development of their children was an important part of their role. Guiding includes making sure the children distinguish right from wrong and that they take responsibility for their relationships, money and other family members. Dads often coupled successful fathering with the ability of their children to integrate into society and act in a responsible manner. For example, one father said:

> I mean seeing them grow as people who hopefully will make a
> contribution to society and hopefully are the kind of kids that
> you can be proud of, you know, that have done something
> worthwhile…that's a matter of trying to bring your children up
> to do what's right and treat people with respect...
> *(Family 6)*

Another suggested that society is 'like a big company that we are in' and children 'are the future generation' of this company (family 23).

Guiding also involved passing on advice and experience, as dad in family 15 described when he was asked about a dad's most important role:

> Oh I would say to be a role model I think but with a bit of
> encouragement to sort of pass on your knowledge. Give them
> your experience.

Micro responsibility

Micro responsibility refers to taking care of the more mundane details of family life. This includes monitoring children's friends, disciplining, planning things, for example sorting out dental and medical appointments, and helping children with their homework. Relatively few fathers were involved in these aspects of their children's lives. Where fathers were involved, they tended to engage with some activities, such as monitoring children's friends, rather than others, such as day-to-day planning.

Monitoring friends

When asked what advice he would give to a father of a teenage daughter, dad in family 6 said:

> To try to understand their friends and the families of their friends and a bit about their background.

Fathers involved in the micro aspects of their children's lives were most likely to be monitoring friends. This meant ensuring that friends were a 'good influence' by vetting them and alerting children to any potential problems rather than dictating which friends to spend time with. For example, in family 5 dad said:

> …one of his [son's] friends was not very nice when he was 11 and we had a lot of problems with him over it because he is very defensive with his friends…I made it clear I didn't like him and we did have a few disagreements, most of his friends are fine.

Some of the dads developed a relationship with the children's friends by being 'jokey dad' so that when the friends came into the family home dad would 'take the mickey' (see below for further discussion of 'jokey dads'). Fathers' monitoring of their children's friends appears to be a continuation of the guiding role fathers adopted as part of their macro responsibilities.

Day-to-day discipline

Discipline generally fell to mothers, although a few parents shared this responsibility. In family 9, for example, the dad explained that mum takes care of this:

> If it comes to there's a telling off to be done, that's her [wife's] department. Because I've never been mega strict with them, I've always thought we will sort it out whatever the problem is.

In some cases, dad was the 'ultimate' disciplinarian and mum would refer things to him either when she couldn't get any further or if it was something 'big'. Again, this was a continuation of the dad's macro responsibility for guiding the children rather than an indication of involvement in day-to-day discipline.

Planning things

Fathers were least likely to be involved in the third area of micro responsibility – planning. A typical example is family 20:

> She [partner] is far better at planning than I am. She worries about things, she says 'why does she have to take all the worry?' And I do see but I am less anxious and I probably leave things to the last minute so I don't plan ahead like she does. She will always think ahead much more than me…

Some families shared planning things equally between mum and dad and this included mums working both full- and part-time and dads working full-time. Family 10 are a good example of parents who shared responsibility for planning which came about when mum went back to work full-time. Dad always took time off work to cover his son's absences from school because of illness or appointments.

In a few cases, dad did most of the planning: in two of these families dad was the main carer and in one, dad was around during the day because he worked nights. For example, in family 23, where dad had recently switched to working part-time and mum to full-time, dad arranged doctors' appointments, maths tuition and 'took the lead' on aspects of his son's academic life.

Who took responsibility for planning appeared to be related to parents' current and previous work commitments. Where mothers did most of the planning, this pattern appeared to have been established over time, with mothers taking on more of this responsibility when they worked fewer hours. Mothers who did most of the planning worked either part-time or full-time, but on the whole they worked fewer hours than their partners.

Homework

Parents were not greatly involved in their children's homework. Some dads' involvement was limited to asking if work had been done or signing the homework book. Other dads got involved when children needed help (usually with maths), although involvement was difficult for dads who were not home from work in time and for dads who believed they lacked the necessary skills to help. For example, one dad felt that his grasp of English was not good enough. The same was true of Dad in family 4:

> I mean to actually help him with his work – I'm afraid I'm not
> much good, 'cos again I'm not that good at clerical stuff. I'm
> good practically, with my hands.

In general, dads are relatively uninvolved in the details of everyday life. The next section explores how much dads take part in activities with their children and to what extent the choice of activity is determined by the dad or the child.

Activities

The amount of time fathers spend in activities with their children has been recognised as an important element of father involvement (Palkovitz, 1997). Three patterns of involvement emerged in our interviews, summarised in Box 3.2. Activities were either 'dad-centred' or 'child-centred', while a small number of fathers were reluctant to be involved in any joint activities. Overall, about half of the dads regularly took part in some type of activity with their child.

Box 3.2 Type of involvement in activities

'Dad-centred'
Dad in family 2 was very interested in rugby. He managed a local rugby team as did his eldest son, and dad's interest had served as a catalyst for other family members' involvement in the local rugby community. His younger son was injured in a match and had to give up playing so dad encouraged him to take up refereeing. However, his son was unhappy as a referee because of the abuse he received. The dad's enthusiasm for rugby and his desire to involve his children made it difficult for the son to explain that he was unhappy being a referee and his dad continued to encourage him in this role, unaware of his son's feelings.

'Child-centred'
There were other families where the interests of the young person acted as a catalyst for dad to get involved. For example, dad in family 18 talked about his enjoyment in 'Getting involved in the activities with your children...Just playing football just doing whatever. Getting involved.' This father had taken up running because his daughter showed an aptitude for it and they both trained together and belonged to the same club.

'Reluctant-activity dad'
For some of the dads there was a clear reluctance either to get involved in joint activities or encourage the children in their own hobbies. Dad from family 1 illustrates this point when talking about his hobby of building models:
'...there's a couple of times he's [son] come out [to help] but normally I'm doing stuff that I can't let him loose on, I mean he could scratch the paintwork and that, so it's a bit awkward...If I do anything I try not to make a mess, but you know what kids are like, it's everywhere except where it should be, so it's a bit awkward. But I would like to get 'em out there, digging the pond, I dug a pond, I put a pond in, they gave me a hand with that, so, but even that, "don't get the mud everywhere!".'

Fathers were generally involved in sport-related activities, but they were also involved in: driving the children to and from events, and to and from school; attending football matches together; playing computer games; and, in one case, chaperoning during acting jobs. Dad in family 21 had planned what he would do with his son when the child was very young:

> We have got two season tickets there since he was five. He and I have been going there since he was five. Every Saturday…and the reason was deliberately a male bonding exercise…I knew if I spent this money on these tickets we would go to football every Saturday. So it was deliberate.

Although more mundane, driving the children around provided an opportunity for dads to chat with their children, as dad in family 11 commented:

> Oh I think it is part of life at the minute isn't it? Like I say, it is a time to have a conversation sometimes. Sometimes we are all in such a rush.

Rather than spending time with one particular child many of the fathers were involved in activities with the whole family (which were usually planned by the mothers). For example, father in family 26 worked away from home for long periods of time and was keen to spend his free time doing things as a family.

'Jokey dads'

Dads often talked about 'mucking around' with the children rather than particular activities. In keeping with previous research that has reported similar findings, we described these fathers as 'jokey dads' (Frosh, Phoenix and Pattman, 2002; Hatten, Vinter and Williams, 2002). One example is dad in family 14. He felt that mucking around with his son showed that they understood each other:

> I'm only strict when I believe I need to be strict. I would rather have the fun, and muck around and have the laughter than have to have the strict bit…he's a good comedian as well. He makes me laugh! But there's a constant repartee all the time. Because we've quite similar senses of humour in that respect.

Mum in family 25 said that the children valued dad acting 'the fool':

> I don't think he has got big social skills in having general
> conversations with people but he does talk to the children a
> lot…there is a lot of communication and a lot of it is amusing to
> the children. It won't necessarily be on serious things most of the
> time, he does like joking with them.

However, for some young people 'jokey dads' were not taken seriously. For example in family 11 dad said he 'takes the mickey out of' his daughter but in her interview she was frustrated that they did not have 'deep conversations' and that she could not take him seriously. In some cases, then, jokey dad acted as a barrier to more serious kinds of communication but in other cases it created the basis on which to build a deeper relationship.

Cognitive and emotional involvement

Cognitive and emotional involvement has come to be seen as an important part of father involvement (Amato, 1994; Pleck and Pleck, 1997). Fathers were asked a number of questions about their mental and emotional involvement, such as: 'What sort of things does your child usually get upset about?' 'Can you usually make him/her feel better?' 'When have you felt particularly close to your son/daughter?' While most fathers described themselves as close to their children, there was considerable variety in their engagement with and understanding of their children's thought life or 'cognitive' world. Overall, fathers were more likely to know what their children were likely to do, or how they would react, than understand what made them 'tick'.

Knowing what son/daughter likes to do

Fathers varied in the extent to which they knew about their children's interests and extracurricular activities. Some fathers had a good idea about the things children liked to do around the house, such as drawing, cooking, and playing computer games, as well as the type of music they listened to and the things they did outside of the home. Family 23 is typical.

> We have become involved in three separate things with
> Anthony…one is ice-skating, because he is good at skating and
> he has been ice-skating for the last three or four years. The other
> is basketball and he plays for a basketball team. The other is
> fencing. And we normally would all trek along together really.

In contrast, other fathers had little idea about their children's 'private world'. For example, Dad in family 9 did not really know how his son spent his free time and believed that this was a 'normal' reflection of his 13-year-old son's growing independence:

> Yes he's just like 'I'm off out' and he's starting to get to that age now where…he'll disappear for some time. He'll be gone for three or four hours at a time no problem.

Understanding the young person

While fathers often knew what their children did, they did not always understand the reasons and meaning behind their moods and behaviour. For example, dad in family 17 felt he could 'read' his daughter well:

> I can tell with Susan, if she's had a nice day or not, when she walks through the door. You know, face like thunder, it means she's had an argument with her Head of Year or something, you know.

However, he did not understand her behaviour. He had no idea why she acted the way she did, offering only vague explanations in terms of her age, or wider social patterns:

> We had, it's just a general lack of respect now from kids of that age, you know. I think Susan is, it's not only my daughter. I think it's society as a whole, you know. That age group. We didn't behave like that as kids.

This father contrasts with others, such as dad in family 21, who felt that he could explain his son's behaviour, or dad in family 8. He felt that he knew his son well and he also articulated the importance of this kind of involvement when asked about giving advice to other parents of teenage boys:

> I would say try and involve yourself as much as you can, in his growing up and in what's happening to him, outside influences, what's going on, just try and be interested really. Try and know him, try and find out what makes him tick. What he likes, what he doesn't like.

The dads who were most cognitively involved, then, were thinking about how to get to know and understand their children. In general, more educated fathers appeared to understand their children better.

Emotional involvement

Existing research has identified the importance of closeness in fathers' involvement (Cabrera and others, 2000). Most fathers were prepared to talk openly about their feelings for their children. For example, in family 20, dad talked about how emotional involvement with his children was central to his parenting:

> I think the most important job of a parent is emotional being there...there is an incredible amount of love in this family...I think a large bit of me really does believe that they [the children] know at a very deep and fundamental level that love is there and if the love is there then the other imperfections will sort themselves out.

Another example is the father in family 14. He felt that his most important job as a dad was 'loving the children' and he was very conscious of his son's need for affection:

> He'll always need support and love. He's sort of sensitive in some ways, he likes, you know, the cuddles from his Mum and his Dad and all that kind of stuff.

In contrast to these fathers, a number of dads could not think of a time when they had felt close to their child and whilst they often said they 'loved' their children they found it difficult to articulate a sense of closeness.

High/low dads

Box 3.3 provides vignettes of different types of involvement and approaches to fathering.

Box 3.3 High/low dads

> **High involvement – Family 21**
>
> Dad rated his involvement as 121 out of a total of 130 on the Inventory of Hawkins and others and his son rated him as 130/130, which indicates a high level of involvement.
>
> Family context: Family 21 was a male breadwinner family. Dad worked quite long hours, although this had been reduced in recent years. Despite this traditional family model, he spent time in the evenings alone with his children as mum did lots of unpaid work that took her out of the house several evenings per week. Both mum and dad were white British and university educated. The son we interviewed was the middle child of three children and the only boy. He was 13 years old.
>
> Dad: He was involved in several activities with his son all of which centred around sport. For example, he goes running with his son and they competed in a race together, and he plays rugby with him in the garden. However, while the child enjoyed doing these things with his dad, they were centred around dad's interests. For example, Dad had not taken an interest in his son's taste in music, rather he had taken his son to concerts that he liked himself to give his son a taste for what he thought was 'better music'. Dad was also cognitively involved – he thought about ways in which to create opportunities for him and his son to spend together so they could get to know each other.
>
> Son: He liked to spend time with his dad and in particular enjoyed playing rugby with him. He also enjoyed chatting about 'stuff that is going on in the world'. He would talk to him about relationship problems: 'I would talk to my dad, they are both easy to talk to, they are good parents.' Kevin also thought his dad thought highly of him: 'he [dad] would say I am a good son. He is a very good dad and he takes me to places.'
>
> **Low involvement – Family 24**
>
> This dad rated his involvement as 80 out of a possible 130 on the Inventory of Hawkins and others and his daughter rated him 81/130. These were the lowest scores of all our interviewees, indicating very low levels of father involvement.
>
> Family context: Mum worked full-time, school term-time only and dad worked full-time. His hours were very long and he was involved in a lot of evening and weekend work. Both mum and dad were white British and university educated. Their daughter was the youngest of three children, with an elder brother and sister. She was 15 years old.
>
> Dad: He did not participate in any activities with his daughter and was, on the whole, quite detached from family life. Dad was distanced from his daughter – which he put down to her 'independent character'. His fathering philosophy was not to interfere. He believed that if he was needed, his daughter would ask for his help. In this sense he was very different from the highly involved father described above who was much more proactive.
>
> Daughter: She was equally distanced from her father and reported quite a difficult relationship with him. She did not think they had much in common and thought that spending time with dad would probably be 'boring'. Instead she valued the time she spent with her friends. However, she also regretted not being closer to her dad and wished that they could talk to each other more easily.

In trying to untangle what father involvement means, it is important to bear in mind that the young people were undergoing a transition to adulthood at the time of the interviews. As a consequence, many of them were spending less time with their parents and more time with their friends, which limited dads' opportunity for involvement. However, there was also evidence that some fathers used this to justify their inability to 'relate' to their children.

Concluding comments

In general, dads were more involved in the macro domain of their children's lives rather than the more mundane details of daily life. In particular, being a dad means 'being there' and being a provider. This is a finding in line with the work of American researchers, such as Cabrera and others (2000) and previous British work (e.g. see Lewis, 2000). Dads were often part of the backdrop of children's lives, only coming to the fore to offer a guiding hand around issues of behaviour, responsibility and friendship. Resident dads knew little about the everyday planning and organisation of their children's lives. This type of passive care raises questions about the challenges faced by non-resident dads in caring for their children. Continuing in a passive caring role is difficult when they are not part of the fabric of the everyday. Similarly, taking on a new role – planning, disciplining, organising – is equally challenging for non-resident dads because they are not familiar with its requirements. These issues are discussed in more detail in Chapter Eight.

Summary points

- Dads in this small sample were more involved in the 'macro' aspects of their children's lives rather than the more mundane details of daily life.

- 'Being there' was an important part of their involvement and one that created a sense of security and stability in family life.

- Where dads were part of the micro aspects of family life, this was most likely to involve monitoring children's friends and least likely to involve planning things.

- 'Jokey dad' was a common way of communicating with children but sometimes this acted as a barrier to other types of communication.

- Many fathers were not involved in regular activities with their children.

- Although dads knew what type of things their children liked to do and how they would react, they had difficulty understanding their teenagers' moods and behaviour.

- Most fathers were emotionally involved to some degree with their children but a number of fathers did not feel 'close' to their children.

4. How involved are dads in their children's lives?

Who did children consider as their mother and father figures?

Who are mum and dad? Table 4.1 indicates the people children described as their mother and father figures. Ninety per cent of children in the sample thought of their biological father as their father figure although 11 per cent of them were living with a stepfather at the time of the interview. Five per cent of children said they had no father figure and 18 per cent were living in a single mother family.

Data in this section are based on the full sample of 2,218 children.

Table 4.1 Children's family circumstances

	Biological mother	Biological father	Stepfather	No father figure
Percentage of children who see respective parent as parent figure (n=2218)	98	90	5	5

How did children rate their father-figures' involvement?

Table 4.2 presents children's ratings of their father-figures' involvement as measured by the Inventory of Involvement (Hawkins and others, 2002). Scores for both biological and social fathers are compared with those for non-resident dads. The average score for resident father figures was 109, compared with an average of 96 for non-resident dads. Statistical tests showed that this was a meaningful difference in children's ratings. However, the means do not portray the whole picture. Scores for both resident and non-resident fathers varied considerably, ranging from 26 to 130[3]. The range shows that some non-resident fathers were rated as highly as some resident fathers. Although the standard deviation – that shows how scores varied in relation to the mean – indicates that children's ratings of non-resident dads varied more widely compared with resident dads.

The factors that explain ratings of father involvement are explored further in Chapter Six. But a simple examination of the means shows how scores varied not only by residence but also by a family's financial circumstances and the level of conflict in the parent's relationship. As Table 4.2 shows, children rated father involvement much lower, on average, in high conflict families and slightly lower in families with poorer socio-economic circumstances, as measured by whether the child received free school meals. In both cases, the difference between the mean scores was statistically meaningful.

Table 4.2 Children's ratings of their father figures based on mean scores on the Inventory of Father Involvement

Mean ratings for father's involvement (Sample of 2,218 children who completed a questionnaire)	Mean rating	Standard deviation+
Resident father figure	109	18.23
Non-resident father figure	96	27.21
Fathers in families receiving free school meals	101*	27.54
Fathers in families not receiving free school meals	105	23.04
Fathers in families with high levels of conflict between parents	98.25**	25.8
Fathers in families with low levels of conflict	109.56	20.26

+ Standard deviation is a measure of how dispersed scores are around the mean.
* $p<0.05$, ** $p<0.001$.

---

[3] The mean father involvement score as reported by children of resident fathers was 109.11 (SD=18.23). The mean father involvement score as reported by children of non-resident fathers was 96.42 (SD=27.21) (t=7.99, df:422.05, p<0.001).

How did children rate different aspects of 'fathering'?

Figure 4.1 shows the mean scores of fathers on the different dimensions of the Inventory (Hawkins and others, 2002) (see Appendix E for details). On eight of the dimensions out of a total possible score of 15 the mean score was 12 or higher for resident fathers. The lowest scores were on 'reading and homework support'. In the interviews some of the fathers admitted they did not have the necessary skills to help. Scores were also lower on 'time and talking together'. Previous studies have shown that 'it is time and talking together' that children most value and which seems hardest for busy parents to achieve (for example, Buchanan, Katz and McCoy, 1999; Katz, Buchanan and Ten Brinke, 1997).

Figure 4.1 Mean scores* in resident and non-resident fathers' survey of different types of involvement as reported by their children

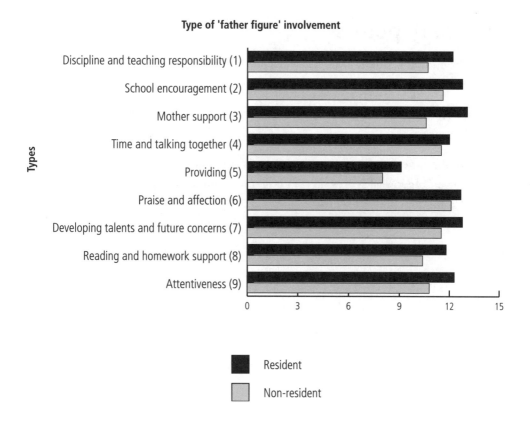

Type of 'father figure' involvement

* Total possible score for all types of father involvement=15, except 'providing' where the total possible score=10.

Although, as we can see, resident fathers were rated higher than non-resident fathers on all nine aspects of involvement, non-resident fathers were also scored relatively highly. However, as the standard deviation scores in Appendix E show, children's ratings of their non-resident fathers varied more widely compared with resident children's ratings. Care needs to be taken in interpreting these figures. Up to 16 per cent of children with non-resident fathers (compared to 6 per cent of children with resident fathers) chose not to record a score on their fathers. This may mean that they had no involvement with the person they thought of as their father. Had these children recorded a score, the overall ratings are likely to have been much lower.

The previous chapter highlighted the role dads play in 'being around' for their children and caring for them in a 'hands-off' way. It is more difficult for non-resident fathers to take this role and this may be reflected in scores on the Inventory. For example, non-resident fathers have less opportunity to show attentiveness, provide support to the resident mother or help with homework, because for much of the time they are simply not there.

Summary points

- Children rated resident fathers' involvement significantly higher than that of non-resident fathers on all nine types of involvement.

- However, ratings also varied according to levels of conflict between parents and family poverty.

- Out of the nine fathering dimensions, both resident and non-resident fathers were given the lowest scores on 'reading and homework support' and on 'time and talking together'.

5. Does being involved matter? Snapshots of father involvement and children's well-being

This chapter examines the relationship between dads' involvement and children's well-being. It is important to stress that the findings do not show that one factor causes another, i.e. that a father's involvement determines a child's well-being. Rather, the findings provide a snapshot of how strongly one factor is associated with another in this sample of fathers.

Children's levels of well-being in the sample

This section looks at children's scores on the Goodman measure of emotional and behavioural difficulties (Strengths and Difficulties Questionnaire). Children can score from between 25 to 75. In a general population 20 per cent of children would be categorised as borderline or experiencing significant emotional and behavioural problems. In our sample, 21 per cent of children fell into this range.

Table 5.1 compares the SDQ scores for children with resident and non-resident fathers. There is a relatively small difference between the mean scores, although this was found to be statistically significant when tested. As Chapter One outlined, children who have experienced their parents' separation are more likely to experience adjustment problems, and this is likely to account for a large proportion of the difference in mean scores. However, the next section explores some of the other factors associated with differences in the well-being of children living with both parents and those in separated families.

Table 5.1 Differences in the mean 'well-being scores' for children with resident and non-resident fathers*

Mean scores and standard deviations for children with resident fathers	Mean scores and standard deviations for children with non-resident fathers
40.31 (6.45)**	41.85 (6.51)

* Higher scores indicate more emotional and behavioural problems.
** $p < 0.001$, $t = 4.17$, df:1620.

What factors are associated with children's well-being in resident father families?

Children's well-being was analysed using a technique called multiple regression. It was used to explore how much of a child's well-being was associated with his or her father's involvement when other factors are taken into account. It also shows how important those factors are or how strongly they are associated. The factors taken into account or 'controlled for' in the analysis are listed in Appendices F and G, and include, for example, poverty and family size. Table 5.2 summarises the details of the analysis.

> Data based on 409 questionnaires returned by resident dads.

Table 5.2 Details of the regression analysis to examine children's well-being and resident fathers' involvement

Whose accounts were included?	Data were drawn from the 409 questionnaires completed by resident fathers. This included biological fathers (369) and social fathers (stepdads (31); adoptive (5); foster (1) and grandfather (2)). Both biological and social fathers were included because children gave them similar ratings on their involvement.
Which variables were used?	The model included data on father involvement (according to dads' reports), parental conflict, dad's mental health and education, and background information such as the age and gender of the child. No measure of mother's involvement was available. A full list is provided in Appendix F.
Which factors were important?	■ dad's involvement ($p < 0.001$) ■ conflict between the parents ($p < 0.001$) ■ female child ($p < 0.01$) ■ father's education ($p < 0.05$) ■ father's mental health ($p < 0.05$) ■ biological father ($p < 0.05$)
How well did the factors explain dads' involvement?	Overall, the model helped to account for 18 per cent of the variance in children's well-being.

Appendix G provides more details about the model and the importance of each factor. The model showed that:

- **A highly involved father** was more likely to have children who were doing well emotionally and behaviourally.
- **High levels of conflict** between the parents were associated with lower levels of well-being in children.
- **Girls** had fewer emotional and behavioural problems than boys.
- **Fathers with mental health difficulties** were more likely to have children with emotional and behavioural difficulties.
- **Biological fathers** were more likely to have well adjusted children.
- **Children of educated fathers** had higher levels of well-being.

Children living with a stepfather had lower levels of emotional and behavioural well-being compared with children living with both biological parents. The finding may not be surprising given the well-established association between the breakdown of parents' relationships and children's well-being. However, it is not possible to establish to what extent parental involvement affects children's well-being or vice versa. Some researchers have found that parents are more involved if they believe the child has an easier disposition (Grolnick and others, 1997) and this may explain the above finding.

Thinking back to Doherty's model (see Figure 1.1, page 2), overall, the findings suggest that factors relating to the characteristics and functioning of the family and its members, such as mental health, conflict, and parental involvement, are more strongly associated with the child's well-being in intact families than the contextual factors included in this study, such as poverty (as measured by free school meals) and family size.

What factors are associated with children's well-being in separated families?

Multiple regression analysis was also used to explore the factors associated with the well-being of children not living with their father. The analysis used data from the questionnaires completed by the 520 teenagers with non-resident fathers because too few non-resident fathers returned questionnaires. Table 5.3 summarises the details of the analysis.

Data based on 520 questionnaires returned by children with non-resident dads.

Table 5.3 Details of the analysis investigating children's well-being in non-resident father families

Whose accounts were included?	Data from the 520 questionnaires completed by young people with non-resident fathers were used in the model.
Which variables were used?	The model included data on dads' involvement and amount of contact as rated by the child; parental conflict (as assessed by the child), mother's involvement, and other background data about the family and child. A full list is provided in Appendix F.
Which factors were important?	Important factors were: ■ a highly involved mother (p<0.001) ■ conflict between the parents (p<0.001) ■ there was a weak link between the length of time since parents separated and children's well-being (p<0.10).
How well did the factors explain dads' involvement?	Overall, the model accounted for 19 per cent of the variance in children's well-being.

Appendix G provides further details about the analysis. The results showed that:

■ **High levels of conflict between parents** were associated with more child adjustment problems.
■ **Highly involved mothers** had children with fewer emotional or behavioural problems.
■ **Time elapsed since the parents' separation** was weakly associated with children's adjustment.

Perhaps the most surprising finding was that non-resident fathers' involvement was not significantly associated with child well-being. This is a surprising result given the importance of father involvement in intact families and given the literature on the role of fathers, although a few other studies (notably Furstenberg, Morgan and Allison, 1987; Kurdek, 1986; Thomas and Forehand, 1993; and Zill, 1988) have reported similar findings. In the case of this study the finding may be explained by some of the methodological issues.

Issues around interpreting the results

The results need to be treated with caution for a number of reasons.

More involved fathers. The rates of contact in the sample are higher than comparative reports, thus these 'in contact' fathers have an opportunity to be involved that is missing for fathers who are not in contact. Moreover, 16 per cent of the children chose not to rate their father's involvement and a further 12 per cent were not in contact. These 'unrated' fathers are likely to be less involved than those fathers who did receive a score.

Independent young people. The interviews revealed that the young people in the sample were at an age when they were becoming more independent, were less likely to be influenced by their fathers and were spending more time with their peers. An association between well-being and non-resident father involvement may be apparent in families with younger children. It may also be the case that positive outcomes of dads' involvement may be more apparent in adulthood – something that can be observed only if children are followed over time.

Using children's reports. Unlike the analysis involving resident fathers, this model was based on children's accounts of factors such as their parents' relationship and it may be that different results would have been obtained had we used fathers' accounts. Moreover, the children's questionnaires did not provide information on fathers' education or mental health, both factors that were important in the analysis of children's well-being in intact families. The results may have been different had it been possible to include the full range of variables for each regression analysis.

Competence versus involvement? Although the Inventory (Hawkins and others, 2002) is designed to measure involvement, the type of questions it asks, such as 'how good dad is at helping with homework', may capture children's sense of how good a job their dad does of fathering as much as how involved he is. That is to say, the measure may reflect dads' competence; so a relatively uninvolved father may be rated highly by his child because they think he does a good job when he is available. Although this is true of resident and non-resident dads, it might be a more important issue for non-resident dads because they are likely to see their children less frequently. Evidence from other studies supports this argument. For example, Furstenberg and Nord (1985) found that 76 per cent of teenagers reported that their fathers were interested in them and loved them even when contact was infrequent.

Other unidentified factors. The model explained only a small amount, 19 per cent, of the variance in children's well-being. A lot remains to be understood about children's well-being in separated families.

Further analysis

Because of the importance of the above finding, further 'interaction analyses' (the details of which are not reported here) were conducted to explore the relationship between each of the factors related to children's well-being. These analyses enable us to determine whether a relationship between two variables, such as involvement and well-being, is confounded by one or more other factors thereby producing misleading results. The analyses addressed the following questions:

1. Is there a stronger association between children's well-being and dads' involvement when mothers are not very involved? There was no evidence to support this.

2. Are children likely to benefit more from their non-resident dad's involvement when parents manage their conflict well? Here we were interested in whether high levels of non-resident involvement could compensate for high levels of couple conflict, in terms of child well-being. We found no evidence to support this.

Concluding comments

These findings are tentative and require further investigation before conclusions can be reached about their reliability and their implications. However, they raise important questions about how contact with fathers following separation should be managed. While ongoing involvement with the non-resident parent may not bring any measurable benefits in the short-term, in most cases, neither is it harmful. Questions arise, however, when contact takes place in a high-conflict environment. An extensive body of research has shown that conflict between parents can be damaging for children both while parents remain together and following separation (e.g. see Reynolds, 2001). Does involvement with the non-resident parent become harmful if the partners cannot manage their conflict effectively?

Summary points

Factors associated with resident fathers' involvement and children's well-being

■ Children were likely to be better adjusted if they were living with their biological father, and their father had good mental health, was well educated and highly involved.

- Children were more likely to be experiencing emotional and behavioural problems if there was conflict between the parents.

- Fathers perceived sons to be more difficult than daughters.

- Overall, factors associated with the character of the family and its members were more closely related to child well-being than the factors associated with the family's environment, such as poverty and family size.

Non-resident fathers' involvement and their children's well-being

- Whereas a resident mother's involvement was significantly associated with greater child well-being, non-resident father involvement in this sample was not. However, caution needs to be exercised in interpreting this finding.

- Children with warring parents were more likely to be experiencing emotional and behavioural difficulties.

6. What factors influence resident fathers' involvement?

The previous chapter examined the links between resident dads' involvement and their children's well-being. This chapter explores the factors that influence resident dads' involvement. The first part presents the findings from the survey and the second part elaborates on the findings by drawing on families' accounts collected in the interviews.

> The data in this section are based on the returns of the 233 mums, dads and children in the 'family sample'.

What factors are associated with resident fathers' involvement? The results of the survey

How was the data analysed?

Multiple regression was again used to explore the factors associated with dads' involvement according to dads' own ratings. The approach to the analysis was underpinned by Doherty's (1998) model, outlined in Chapter One, which suggests involvement is affected by: the family context, the characteristics of each member of the family and the relationship between the parents.

Explaining dads' involvement according to their own ratings

Table 6.1 provides details of the regression model.

Table 6.1 Details of the analysis to explore dads' involvement using dads' ratings

Whose accounts were included?	Data from the questionnaires of the 233 fathers, mothers and children living together were included. Both biological and social fathers were included because children gave them similar ratings on their involvement.
Which variables were used?	The analysis used fathers' accounts of their involvement and their reports about the family and all its members. The variables included in the model are listed in Appendix F.
Which factors were important?	■ father's gender attitudes (p<0.01) ■ mother's involvement (p<0.01) ■ children's emotional and behavioural well-being (p<0.05) ■ there was a weak link between father's self-esteem and involvement (p<0.10).
How well did the factors explain dads' involvement?	Overall, the model accounted for 35 per cent of the variance in dads' involvement.

Appendix G provides further details about the model and the strength of factors associated with dads' involvement. Only three factors were meaningful in a statistical sense. These were:

■ **Mother's involvement.** Fathers were more likely to play an active part in their children's upbringing when mothers were also very involved.

■ **Father's gender equality attitudes.** Fathers with more liberal attitudes to men's and women's roles were more likely to be involved with their children.

■ **Children's well-being.** Where children were rated by their fathers as experiencing emotional and behavioural difficulties dads were less likely to be involved. That is to say, the more difficult fathers thought their children were, the less likely they were to play a significant role at home.

A regression analysis was also run using data from the 233 children's questionnaires in the 'family sample'. The analysis used children's accounts of their fathers' involvement. The findings, not reported here, echoed those of the first model. As with the previous model, the level of mum's involvement predicted dad's involvement, and children's self-esteem was found to be important, as opposed to the more general measure of children's emotional and behavioural well-being.

One factor that was not included in the analysis was marital status. This may have explained some of the differences in fathers' involvement, as recent research has found that being married accounted for differences in stepfathers' involvement with their stepchildren (Hofferth and Anderson, 2003). However, marital status was not explored in this study because of the range of family forms represented in the sample.

But what underlies the factors associated with involvement?

The regression analysis identified which factors explain why some dads are more involved than others. But they also raise the question of what circumstances or characteristics are associated with these factors? For example, what determines whether mum is involved? What explains dad's attitudes to 'his and her' roles? These questions were explored using a different type of regression technique – a path analysis stepwise regression, but the technical details are not reported here.

Table 6.2 The characteristics underlying the three factors associated with dads' involvement

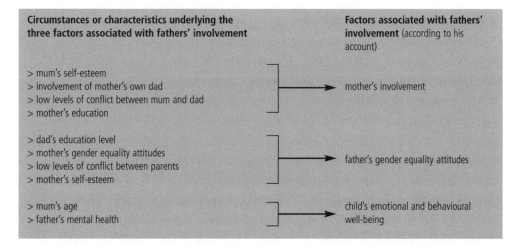

Circumstances or characteristics underlying the three factors associated with fathers' involvement	Factors associated with fathers' involvement (according to his account)
> mum's self-esteem > involvement of mother's own dad > low levels of conflict between mum and dad > mother's education	mother's involvement
> dad's education level > mother's gender equality attitudes > low levels of conflict between parents > mother's self-esteem	father's gender equality attitudes
> mum's age > father's mental health	child's emotional and behavioural well-being

Factors associated with mothers' involvement

■ **Mums with high self-esteem** were more likely to be involved. Other researchers have reported similar findings (van Bakel and Riksen-Walraven, 2002; Volling and Belsky, 1991).

■ **Mums whose own fathers had been involved** were more likely to be involved in the child's upbringing. Previous research has not found this association, although it has found that fathers are more likely to be involved if their dads were involved (Roberts, Block and Block, 1984).

■ **Low levels of conflict between the parents** were associated with mums being more involved (from the dad's perspective).

■ **The lower the mum's educational attainment** the more likely she was to be involved. This result is slightly surprising because more educated fathers were more involved with their children.

Factors associated with fathers' gender equality attitudes

■ **Better educated fathers** were more likely to hold more egalitarian attitudes.

■ **Mums with egalitarian gender attitudes** were more likely to have partners with similar views.

■ **Low levels of conflict between the parents** (according to father's report) were associated with fathers holding a more egalitarian outlook.

■ **Mothers had poorer self-esteem** where fathers were more egalitarian. This is a slightly surprising result that we cannot explain.

Factors associated with children's well-being

■ **Fathers with poorer mental health** were more likely to rate their children as having adjustment problems.

■ **Fathers with more egalitarian gender attitudes** were less likely to have children with emotional and behavioural problems.

■ **The younger the mother** the more likely it was that the children were experiencing emotional and behavioural difficulties, according to their father.

It is important to note that the path analysis does not show whether one factor caused another. However, the results do show that families with an involved father share a collection of characteristics that distinguish them from families where dad is not very involved. Families are spread along a continuum of parental involvement and emotional resources. At one end of the spectrum are more 'child-centred' families. In these families, dad is likely to be well-educated, both parents are involved with the children and likely to hold egalitarian attitudes, have high levels of self-esteem and be part of a supportive and amicable relationship. Surprisingly, the analysis indicated that more poorly educated mothers are more likely to be involved. This finding is inconsistent with the other results and is one that requires further investigation.

At the other end of the spectrum are more 'adult-centred' families who have fewer resources available to them. In these families, both mum and dad are not very involved, argue frequently and have inequitable gender attitudes. Moreover, dad is likely to be poorly educated and mum, dad and the children are likely to be suffering from low self-esteem or mental health difficulties.

What factors are associated with resident fathers' involvement? Findings from the in-depth interviews

The next section explores the accounts of 26 families about the circumstances that shape dads' participation at home. The accounts confirm and expand the findings of the survey in pointing to the importance of mother, father and child characteristics. However, the findings also emphasise the importance of family context, such as employment patterns – issues that were not significant in the survey data. The role of mothers' involvement was also less prominent in the interviews, although the accounts did highlight the importance of the relationship between the parents, which acts as a vehicle for enabling dads to be involved.

> The data in this section are based on interviews with the members of 26 intact families.

The sample comprised intact families, with at least one employed parent and where both parents and the child had completed a questionnaire and agreed to be interviewed. Parents are unlikely to have agreed to participate in the research if they were experiencing significant parenting problems, marital difficulties or other issues that they may have preferred not to discuss in an interview. These issues should be borne in mind when reading the next section.

Factors related to the father's characteristics

Fathers' skills and confidence

In line with previous research (Pleck, 1997), the interviews revealed that some fathers' involvement was affected by a lack of skills and confidence in both education and communication. For example, a number of fathers talked about how they struggled to help with their children's homework. In some cases fathers were stuck on particular subjects, while others felt unable to help with any homework subject. Such a lack of confidence was quite common among this group of fathers but it often extended beyond homework to more general caring aspects of family life. Mum in family 5, for example, mentioned that dad had not taken much responsibility for caring for the children when they were very young because of his lack of confidence:

> It would've been nice, you know, when he [son] was younger for
> him [husband] to have been able to take him out to the park or
> something like that. That would've been nice. He just wasn't that
> kind of confident person really.

Father in family 3 was one of the least involved dads in the qualitative sample and he felt his lack of confidence was a hindrance to his involvement:

> **I:** If you could change anything about the way you are as a dad,
> what would you change?
> **R:** Eh (long pause) I'd probably just get more confident with
> them.

Poor communication skills were also an issue for some fathers. This made building a relationship between father and child difficult and made it hard for fathers to help their children talk about problems and issues. Dad in family 11 said:

> …I am just not a very good talker, and I find that with the kids as
> well really.

Communication in family 12 between father, who was born overseas, and son, who was born in the UK, was affected by dad's lack of 'cultural knowledge':

> The cultural gap is very, very, um, is the enemy with him
> [son]…I'm speaking with a different accent they're [his
> children] not happy with it…they're not impressed with me, with
> my way of life…we don't talk about my background where I come
> from. They don't want to know.

'Natural' fathering

Fathers' involvement was also affected by their beliefs about what being a father means. Dads often talked about their approach using terms such as 'natural', which meant fathering was something fixed and unchanging that could not be taught or learnt. For example, dad in family 17 talked about 'learning' to be a dad:

> I can't see how people can teach you to be a dad, you know it
> comes naturally if you're a good dad, or a bad dad, it just comes
> naturally…it all comes down to what sort of person you are, and
> you know, it comes naturally.

Others researchers, such as Lupton and Barclay (1997) in their study of Australian fathers, have found that fathers believe things come naturally to them, but in contrast to our sample, the Australian fathers also saw a place for seeking knowledge and learning. Our sample of dads believed that overcoming particular characteristics meant somehow denying your 'true self'. Dad in family 10 exemplifies these beliefs:

> ...I think your personality moulds the way you are, if you've got
> to work at being or behaving in a particular way, it's false.

This preference for doing what 'comes naturally' forms the basis of a parenting philosophy for this group of fathers. The way in which fathers use this natural discourse to explain their behaviour means that promoting a child-centred approach to fathering is difficult if the child's and father's interests do not 'naturally' match, as we saw in Chapter Three.

Child factors

The survey findings indicated that fathers are less likely to be involved where they perceive the child to have emotional and behavioural difficulties. The interviews confirmed and expanded these findings and also identified other important factors, including the child's age, transition to independence, and gender.

Disposition

Some fathers talked about communication problems and the difficulties of coping with the moods and disposition of their teenage children. Father in family 17 found his teenage daughter's temperament difficult. Dad in family 19 found it difficult to communicate with his 15-year-old son because he no longer related to 'jokey dad'. Mum in family 19 confirmed their son's rather critical view of his father:

> He calls his dad a pillock! (laugh) You know, it's that age when
> they're very critical.

Mum in family 9 said that their son did not talk to them very much and she put this down to his current mood:

> At the moment because he is 13 now, he goes to school, he
> comes home, he gets changed, he grabs a sandwich, he doesn't
> get in the house until – I like him to be in before it's dark, he

> comes in, has his dinner and then he'll go upstairs and play on
> the computer. He doesn't really talk, even about his homework,
> he used to, he doesn't now.

Similarly, in family 21 communication between father and son had become increasingly strained and his son had started to spend more time with his 'mates'.

It is clear, then, that for these fathers the particular disposition of teenage children raised difficulties for them, particularly in terms of communication. However, three of these four dads were not very involved in other areas of their children's lives and this exacerbated communication difficulties.

Fathers in families where children were not perceived to be difficult reported little or no conflict. Dad in family 23, is one example:

> ...we don't have a lot of conflict about him wanting to do things
> that we tell him he can't do really. I mean he doesn't go out to
> parties, he doesn't go out drinking...and actually he is quite
> forgiving really. If he gets sent to bed or something he doesn't
> seem to hold it against you the next morning.

For the majority of our interviewees there was a certain level of 'mis-communication' with young people but in more extreme cases communication had broken down and fathers were at a loss as to how to handle the situation.

Age and independence

The majority of our families recognised that they were at a crossroads with their teenage children. The young people's transition to adulthood often left fathers feeling 'left behind' and redundant. Father in family 2 said:

> I am not needed as much that is the only thing I notice. I don't
> like that and that is part of growing up, I am not needed
> nowhere near as much as I used to be.

His son also talked about how he spent less time with his father now, because: '...you just go out with your mates'.

Dad in family 15 described how he found the growing independence of his daughter difficult:

> ...you don't like to see your daughter grow up and become
> independent but you don't want to be in their face all the
> time...I encourage the independence but at the same time I am
> reluctant to let go.

He went on to say:

> ...we would sit down and watch a film together but again she will
> sometimes prefer to go out with her friends rather than sit down
> and watch a video. I think in the past year she has particularly
> become more independent and I have taken one step back...

In general, the transition to independence meant that fathers were less involved with their children than they had been in the past. However, as some avenues of involvement were perhaps closing down, fathering a teenage son or daughter could require fathers to be more cognitively involved as they learnt to deal with emerging adults.

Gender

It is surprising that the survey did not identify a link between father involvement and child gender given the large body of evidence for such an association (Cabrera and others, 2000; Pleck, 1997; Volling and Belsky, 1991). The interviews, however, revealed great variation in the extent to which gender affected involvement. In some families, the young person's gender affected fathers' understanding and cognitive involvement. Father in family 11, for example, described the difficulties he had in understanding his daughter:

> **I:** It is hard work trying to understand a teenage daughter.
> **R:** Do you think it is different from your son?
> **I:** Oh yes, because my son is completely laid back and me and
> him are on the same wavelength really.

The absence of a shared gender identity, then, also affected fathers' ability to empathise with their children. As this dad went on to say:

> ...there are lots of things a father can't do with a daughter, there
> are lots of personal things, female things, I mean you obviously
> know about it, but you can't be on the same wavelength or

> discuss those problems because you don't experience them...
> being a mere mortal man I don't know what goes through their
> [teenage daughters] heads.

In other cases, fathers were less likely to share interests with their daughters than their sons. For example, dad in family 6 had more common interests, centred around sport, with his sons than with his daughter.

Some parents also felt that boys benefited more than girls from having a father figure around, as mum in family 19 explained:

> ...it doesn't seem to matter with the girls somehow. I mean, you
> know, he was just 'Dad' to them, and the authority thing didn't
> seem to matter. It matters much more with him [son].

Parental gender was also important for the children. Almost without exception the young people interviewed said they would talk to their mother before their father if they were upset about something or wanted to discuss personal issues – this was equally true of boys and girls.

Just under half of fathers interviewed, then, perceived gender to be an important factor that affected different dimensions of their involvement. Fathers' ideas about shared gender identities are another aspect of their beliefs about fathering as something fixed. In this case, being a different sex from their child meant they felt they had less in common with them and were unable to do things together.

Cooperative parenting

The survey revealed important links between dads' involvement and the relationship between the parents, in keeping with the findings of previous research (Flouri and Buchanan, 2003; Doherty, Kouneski and Erickson, 1998; McBride and Rane, 1998; Abidin and Brunner, 1995). Research has also shown that the relationship between the parents, or what we refer to as the cooperative parenting relationship[4], has a greater influence on fathering than mothering (Eggebeen and Knoester, 2001; Gerson, 1993). Our in-depth interviews also revealed that the relationship between the parents was an important factor in father involvement. Families fell on different points on a continuum of involvement whereby fathers were more involved the more they were part of a mutually supportive and cooperative parenting partnership. The process by which the relationship affected dads' involvement was complex and explored in detail in the interviews, which covered: maternal gatekeeping and

---

[4] We have used the term 'cooperative parenting' to refer to the relationship between the mother and the father as revealed in the qualitative data. In much quantitative research the term 'co-parental relationship' is often used; however, because this is understood in the existing psychology literature in a technical, quantitative sense (see for example Abidin and Brunner, 1995; McBride and Rane, 1998), we have used a different term when discussing the qualitative data to signify that we are discussing the relationship between parents in a more general sense.

enabling roles; how parents shared out responsibilities for family life, and how and in what ways parents supported each other. It is important to bear in mind when reading the following section that the interviews were conducted with intact families with low levels of conflict.

Enabling

'Maternal gatekeeping', a term coined in previous research, describes families where the mother exerts control over the family and decides when their partner's involvement is or is not required (e.g. see Lewis, 2000). We found little evidence of any maternal gatekeeping in the families we interviewed. However, mothers were trying to facilitate fathers' involvement, with varying levels of success. For example, father in family 3 described how his partner often suggested things for him to do with the children:

> I find it (pause) strange that she's [partner] always saying, 'You could do this with the kids' and 'You could do that with the kids', and I just think, 'Well, if I can do it, why can't you do it?' (laugh) You know, 'If you've a good idea, why don't you go and do it?'

Clearly, he was resisting mum's attempts to get him involved, although in other families, mothers' attempts were more successful. For example, mum in family 8 said she encouraged her husband and son to talk to each other. Dad in family 8 confirmed mum's enabling role:

> I think women are generally much more perceptive than men with things that need to be done. I need telling that they need doing. But once I'm told, I'll do it.

For the majority of the families we interviewed, however, mum did not play an enabling role and two mothers openly rejected playing this role. When discussing how she would like her husband to play a more active part with their daughter, mum in family 7 said:

> ...when he has had his tea, he is tired, so I don't try to push him too much on that...although at the same time I think it would be nice if he did spend a little bit more time with her [daughter].

Mutual support

The qualitative data provided the opportunity to explore how the parental relationship linked to fathering. Rather than determine dads' involvement, the interviews paint a picture of the parental relationship as a backdrop for parenting. In the majority of families there was an association between the couple relationship and dad's involvement; where the parents enjoyed a mutually supportive co-parental relationship dads were more likely to be involved, and fathers were less likely to be involved if they were in a less supportive relationship.

In half of the families we interviewed, father involvement was high and the parents were supportive of each other in their 'parenting project'. Family 20 exemplifies this 'cooperative parenting', as mum explained:

> ...we respect each other's differences, basically I think we work quite well as parents...we do disagree sometimes but I think we hopefully show that we do discuss it and then come to an agreement.

Dad in family 23 felt that the relationship with his wife acts as a model for their son and he believed it was important that they work well together:

> The way we behave and the way we act would influence the way he thinks a relationship should be carried on.

In other families, such as family 21, support was vital in working out how to deal with teenage demands.

> I think we discuss it because we sort of cling to each other, for mutual support I think. We put together ideas and there are some things that William will feel very strongly about and there will be things that I feel very strongly about.

In nine families, fathers were less involved and the parents had a less mutually supportive and cooperative co-parental relationship. In family 25, for example, mum felt that her husband did not support her in her role as a parent:

> 'Supporting you as a parent'...I am not sure he stops and thinks about this as being a very serious question a lot of the time...I do feel that I am undermined a lot in that he might make a joke about me or I might say something and behind my back he will you know, laugh and point, in front of the children, so the children can see, so it is all going on behind my back and I feel like I am being treated like another child.

In family 1, mum reported difficulty setting down guidelines for the children because her husband broke them first:

> We have attempted to sit at the table for the evening meal, and it
> hasn't gone too well... I would put them all down and we would
> all sit at the table. I didn't care what was on the television and
> Tim [husband] has always been the first one to break the rule so,
> and they will say 'well why have we got to sit at the table and dad
> is watching the film?'

Dad's behaviour, then, meant that mum's new ideas were not supported. They did not discuss with each other why it might be worth sitting down at the table for dinner. Such a lack of communication was quite typical of the families where there was a lack of mutual support combined with lower levels of father involvement. Mums' strategies for facilitating their partners' involvement echo the findings of the survey analysis in highlighting the role of mothers' involvement as a factor in dads' participation at home.

Contextual factors

Employment

The context in which the family operates has an important influence on parenting, but particularly on the father–child relationship (Doherty, Kouneski and Erickson, 1998). Fathers' work commitments affected how much time they could spend with the children. For example, a few dads reluctantly took overtime when it was offered because they needed the extra money. Other dads had worked extra hours to further their career. In both cases working overtime affects the important 'being there' factor discussed in Chapter Three.

Seven of the dads worked shifts and this affected their involvement in different ways. Father in family 4, for example, rarely saw his child when he worked on late shifts. However, shift work also meant fathers could be around at important times of the day. Dad in family 22 worked the longest hours (72 hours per week) in two shifts per day. However, this working pattern meant that he was at home when the children left for school and when they came home again. He valued spending this time with them:

> I normally do shopping and go to school to see the little one [his
> youngest daughter]. I know she can come home alone.
> I thought it is much nicer to meet her, I mean it doesn't cost me
> much. I come past there about 2.30pm, I always wait for her in
> my car. I arrive here [home] and we have toast and tea all
> together.

Six fathers were self-employed working a variety of hours. They made use of the flexibility this afforded. For example, father in family 23 was able to fit meetings around family life which meant he was there before and after school:

> ...he [son] has got a key and can let himself in if he wants to,
> but I think it is not very nice to come home to a deserted house.
> I mean it is nice to come home and have someone to talk to
> when you are here, so I will try and be here normally.

Two families had moved several times because of fathers' work commitments and this affected their involvement. In family 6 the son had not moved with the family so he could complete his education and in the other case dad was about to be separated from his family for 18 months so that his children's education was not disrupted again. Despite the distance, dad in family 6 regularly phoned and the child often came home for visits.

A few fathers talked about their employers' family-friendly approach. For example, Dad in family 20 said:

> I work for a Swedish company so it is very different, very different
> [from his previous job]...they kind of expect you to take care of
> the family and my male contemporaries will – if they have to take
> kids to school – they will come in at 10 o'clock and do whatever
> has to be done, so it's a very different attitude. It's great fun.

Overall, flexible work hours were extremely valued by those who had access to such arrangements. In contrast, employment acted as a barrier to involvement for those fathers who travelled frequently and missed both day-to-day family life and significant family events. Long hours were also problematic. Dads in these families were described by mums and their children as 'tired' or 'stressed' which precluded them from getting involved in the detail of family life.

Social support

When asked 'who would they talk to about dad things' most fathers said they would talk to their wives or partners and most mothers confirmed this. For example, in family 16 dad would talk to his wife rather than his friends:

> **I:** So if you wanted to talk to somebody about dad things, who would you talk to? Say you had a problem with one of the children and you wanted to talk to your friend about it?
> **R:** I wouldn't talk to my friends, I'd talk to my wife.

Close friendship networks among most fathers, then, were notable by their absence. However, a minority of fathers talked about using their friends and/or family as a support network, in keeping with previous research (McBride and others, in press). Dad in family 2 was friendly with several local fathers. They often took the children on outings without wives or partners. In these cases, the network enhanced dads' involvement. For example, they organised local sport tournaments, particularly during the summer holidays, in which local children could participate.

Dad in family 9 said he often discussed family life with his work friends. In family 14, dad chatted about family issues with his 'golfing' friends:

> **R:** Oh yeah, yeah! We talk constantly, we go out for a drink, there's about five of us go out, or we're walking around the golf course, we're constantly saying, 'You won't believe what's happened?'
> **I:** Comparing?
> **R:** Yeah, you do compare notes, I suppose in some ways you try and pick up, 'I can use that' sort of thing, you know.

He commented on the value of such support because it was easier to cope when knowing other people were experiencing similar issues.

Concluding comments

The survey and the in-depth interviews provide a complementary insight into dads' involvement with their children. When considering the findings it is worth remembering that the interviewees could be described as a select sample – low in conflict, in full-employment, and cooperative enough that each family member was willing to be interviewed. The sub-sample involved in the survey analysis in this chapter are also likely to be more select than the rest of the sample because both parents are sufficiently engaged in family life to take the time to complete the questionnaire given to them by their child.

The survey analysis identified families who varied in the level of parental involvement they enjoyed and in the range of social and emotional resources available to them. The interviews paint a fuller picture of these families and the factors identified by the survey as important to fathering. According to the survey, involved dads are likely to be well-educated, part of an amicable relationship with a partner who is also involved with the children and they are likely to share an egalitarian outlook. The interviews added to this picture, showing how the parents' relationship helped fathers be involved because of the mutual support each spouse provided. The interviews also suggested that fathers are likely to be more involved with children who have an easier disposition. While the survey highlighted the importance of mum's self-esteem, the interviews revealed that more confident dads who were more skilled in communication felt more able to get involved with their kids. Some dads also held strong views about fathering as something that comes naturally and that is not amenable to change. For fathers lacking confidence these fixed views make it difficult to offer support or interventions that might improve their skills and confidence.

At the other end of the spectrum were more 'adult-centred' families where neither parent was very involved with the children because they were preoccupied by the conflict and emotional problems in their own lives. According to the survey, these identified parents were less likely to have succeeded in their education, had lower levels of confidence and self-esteem and were likely to be suffering from mental health difficulties. Their children were also more likely to be experiencing adjustment problems. Moreover, the interviews also pointed to the difficulties dads faced in getting involved in this 'teenage' phase of their children's lives. Children who found the transition to adulthood more difficult than their peers were even less likely to have the involvement of their father. Uninvolved dads were also more likely to be in conflict with their partner and so seemed to lack the supportive relationship that the interviews showed boosted dads' confidence in and knowledge of how to get involved.

Both the survey and the interviews highlighted the significant role of the parents' relationship in facilitating dads' involvement. Helping dads also means helping couples. But what should that help look like? The policy issues around the implications of this and other findings are discussed in more detail in Chapter Eight, but their implementation is inevitably constrained by fathers' clear ideas about the 'natural' and 'unlearned' nature of parenting.

Summary points

Findings from the survey

- Resident father-figures' involvement with their adolescent children was related to mothers' involvement. The story was the same according to mothers, fathers and children.

- From the fathers' responses, fathers were more likely to be involved if they held egalitarian gender role attitudes.

- Fathers were less likely to be involved where children exhibited emotional and behavioural problems (according to the fathers' report).

- High self-esteem in mothers (as indicated by mothers' responses) and in children (as indicated by children's responses) was associated with greater father involvement.

- Overall the findings suggest that directly or indirectly there are important links between different factors that are associated with father involvement.

- On the one hand there are more 'child-centred' families where fathers are more flexible about their roles and more highly educated and where both parents have high levels of self-esteem and an amicable and supportive relationship.

- At the other end of the spectrum, there are more adult-centred families in which neither parent is very involved, the parents are not getting on well, mothers have low self-esteem, dads have inflexible gender role attitudes and, along with their children, are likely to be experiencing mental health problems.

Findings from the interviews

- For a number of dads, their involvement was hindered by a lack of skills and confidence.

- Approaches to fathering were understood as 'natural' by some fathers and thus not very amenable to change.

- Because of gender differences, some dads were less likely to be involved in activities with their daughters and, in a few cases, there was a lack of mutual understanding.

- Fathers were more likely to be involved if they were part of a cooperative partnership with their spouse.

■ The small number of fathers working for employers with family-friendly policies valued the flexibility and time it afforded them. Shift-work or self-employment created flexibility for some of the other dads.

■ The interviews were with a 'select' group of parents who are likely to be more involved with their children and get on better as a couple than other parents.

7. How does being a non-resident father affect involvement?

As the previous chapter revealed, resident dads' involvement is strongly influenced by the relationship with the mother. This chapter looks at the factors associated with non-resident dads' involvement, including the role of the revised parenting relationship following separation or divorce. Before examining involvement the chapter looks at the factors influencing contact – a necessary precursor to fathers' involvement.

> The data are from the 520 questionnaires completed by children with non-resident fathers.

Levels of contact

The reports of contact are based on the accounts of children who completed the questionnaire. It is likely that, because they completed the questionnaire, either they are more positive about their father or their father has more contact with them, or both. Moreover, 16 per cent of children with non-resident fathers did not give a score on their father figure and 12 per cent had never lived with their father, which means there were few ratings for 'less involved' dads. It is likely, therefore, that the results are pertinent for children who have more contact with non-resident fathers than those who have little or none.

Table 7.1 Levels of contact between non-resident father and child

Type of contact	Percentage of children reporting particular types of contact
Informal	
Telephone	69
Letters	17
Gifts	58
Face-to-face	
At least once a week	43
Once a month	14
Every three months	25

Table 7.1 summarises levels of contact in the sample. Levels of contact for the sample are relatively high compared to other studies, which have found that over half of fathers did not remain in contact (see Maclean and Eekelaar, 1997). However, the high levels of contact for this group are not surprising given the nature of the sample.

What factors are associated with levels of contact between the non-resident dad and his child?

As in previous chapters multiple regression was used to explore the factors associated with non-resident dads' contact with their children. Table 7.2 summarises the details of the regression analysis.

Table 7.2 Details of the analysis to explore non-resident dads' contact with their children

Whose accounts were included?	The analysis utilised data from the 520 questionnaires completed by children who nominated their non-resident father as their father figure.
Which variables were used?	Children's accounts of contact were used along with their reports of conflict between parents*, time since their parents separated, and standard measures such as age and gender. A full list is provided in Appendix F.
Which factors were important?	The most important factor was: ■ time since parents separated (p<0.001) ■ there was a weak link between conflict between parents and contact (p<0.10).
How well did the factors explain dads' involvement?	Overall, the model accounted for just 6 per cent of the variance in contact levels.

* As 11 per cent of children were living with a step-parent their reports of conflict may relate to their mother and stepfather rather than mother and non-resident father.

Appendix G contains further details about the regression analysis, including the strength of association. The regression shows that the longer fathers have been separated from their ex-partner the less frequently they see their children. This is the case regardless of the child's age. There was a weak link between parental conflict and infrequent contact. It is surprising that this association was not stronger given that other research has found that father contact is related to the quality of his relationship with the child's mother (Amato and Rezac, 1994). However, the model explained only a small proportion, i.e. just 6 per cent, of the factors that affect contact, and there are likely to be many other factors that influence contact levels.

What factors are associated with non-resident dads' involvement?

Multiple regression was also used to explore the factors associated with non-resident dads' involvement. The details are summarised in Table 7.3.

Table 7.3 Details of the regression analysis of non-resident dads' involvement

Whose accounts were included?	Information from the 520 questionnaires completed by children who nominated their non-resident father as their father figure was included in the model.
Which variables were used?*	Children's accounts of contact were used along with their reports of conflict between parents, time since their parents separated, and standard measures such as age, gender and receipt of free school meals. A full list is provided in Appendix F.
Which factors were important?	The following factors were important: ■ levels of conflict between parents (according to the child) (p<0.01) ■ mum's involvement (p<0.001) ■ there was a weak link between time since parents separated and non-resident dads' involvement (p<0.10).
How well did the factors explain dads' involvement?	Overall, the model accounted for 19 per cent of the variance in non-resident dads' involvement.

* Children's well-being was not included because it was the main variable in the analysis of well-being and the models would have been too similar.

Appendix G contains further details about the model. Only two factors were found to be significant:

■ as with resident fathers, dads are more likely to be involved when **mum is highly involved**;
■ **conflict between the parents** was associated with less father involvement.

Conclusions

The findings highlight the importance of the couple relationship in influencing dads' involvement. In particular, conflict between parents mitigates against dads taking a part in their children's lives. This is borne out by the findings of other studies (for example, see Trinder, Beek and Connolly, 2002). As is the case with resident dads, mum's involvement is also important in promoting involvement. It is less clear, however, how mum's involvement relates to the parents' relationship. For example, Carlson and McLanahan (2001) found that fathers who communicate effectively with the child's mother have greater access to information about, and therefore a greater understanding of, the child. This may increase his involvement with the child. But it may also be that because a mother is involved with a child and has a child-centred approach, she may be more willing to facilitate involvement with the non-resident father.

Summary points

■ Non-resident fathers were more likely to be involved if the mother was highly involved and, as with contact, if the parents had recently separated.

■ Fathers were less likely to be involved in cases of conflict between partners.

■ These findings need to be treated with caution given the nature of the sample, the reliance on children's reports and the number of children with non-resident dads who did not give a rating.

8. Policy dilemmas

There is enormous pressure on policy makers to respond to the findings of each new research study often in the context of contradictory findings covering complex and wide-ranging issues. Given these difficulties, this chapter is an exploration of policy 'dilemmas' rather than policy 'implications'.

Resident fathers

Resident dads are more involved with their offspring than non-resident fathers. Their involvement is partly facilitated by their physical presence. According to the in-depth interviews, being involved is partly about 'being there' and being there in a more passive way than other researchers have noted in the past (Warin and others, 1999).

The nature of fathers' involvement reflects cultural shifts of recent decades and contains elements of the old and the new. The interviews reveal that family members continue to believe that a father's role is to act as guide and guardian to the children and to provide for the family, echoing other research (Warin and others, 1999). However, dads were less involved in daily life and some fathers lacked confidence in their caring and communication skills. The survey shows that dads' involvement is linked to their gender attitudes. Fathers with a more egalitarian outlook are more likely to be involved with their children. The interviews, however, suggest that involvement is hampered by dads' work commitments and the time they can be at home (see Chapter Six). As the roles, expectations and demands on fathers are in flux, policy may be most helpful if it aims to ease the process of cultural change by creating a climate that facilitates family-friendly working practices.

According to the survey analysis, dads' involvement is entwined with that of mothers. The more involved the mother, the more likely the father was to be involved. Helping dads to be involved with their children, therefore, partly means helping mothers in their parenting.

Spousal relationship

While dads need mothers to be involved, mums need the couple relationship to be functioning well. Mothers' involvement is affected by conflict and both parents' involvement is affected by the support they receive from one another (see Chapter Six). A number of researchers have also identified the important influence of the spousal relationship on parenting (Coiro and Emery, 1998; Hetherington and Stanley-Hagan, 1997; Lewis, Maka and Papacosta, 1997).

Dads' involvement with difficult children

Dads are less likely to be involved with their children when the latter display emotional and behavioural difficulties (see Chapter Six). The interviews revealed that fathers often struggle to be involved with their children during the teenage years as children strive to establish their independence. Children with adjustment difficulties, who are therefore most likely to need their parents' nurturing and care, are likely to become increasingly distanced from their fathers during their adolescence.

A continuum of parental involvement and family well-being

Chapter Six described the combination of factors identified in the survey analysis that are directly and indirectly associated with fathers' involvement. Families can be conceptualised along a continuum of parental involvement and family resources. At one end of the spectrum are 'child-centred' families that have highly involved parents with egalitarian attitudes, high levels of self-esteem and a supportive and amicable relationship. Children in these families are likely to be doing well emotionally and behaviourally (see Chapter Six). Surprisingly, more poorly educated mothers were found to be more involved. This is inconsistent with the other findings and requires further investigation.

At the other end of the spectrum are more 'adult-centred' families characterised by relatively uninvolved parents who argue frequently and have inequitable gender attitudes. In which case, mum is likely to bear the brunt of looking after the home and the children. Moreover, dad is likely to be poorly educated and mum, dad and children are likely to be suffering from low self-esteem or mental health difficulties. Children in these families are likely to be poorly adjusted (see Chapter Six). The social and emotional difficulties these parents face may make it difficult for them to focus on their children.

The family's socio-economic circumstances were not found to be important in distinguishing between 'child-centred' or 'adult-centred' families, although the proxy measure for poverty, i.e. free school meals, may not have been sufficiently sensitive to differentiate.

The findings point to vulnerable families caught in a cycle of difficulties. This is especially so when we consider that mothers were more likely to be involved if their own fathers had been involved in their upbringing and other research has suggested that a dad's involvement is linked to his experiences with his own father (Roberts, Block and Block, 1984). The findings also point to the value of holistic intervention. Promoting better father–child relationships is about enhancing whole family well-being. Targeting one problem or one family relationship is not enough. Potential avenues for intervention include:

- helping parents to reduce conflict and build a mutually supportive relationship;
- measures to improve children's mental health;
- helping mothers to be involved and to understand how their behaviour impacts dads' involvement;
- helping dads to develop their confidence and communication skills.

While it is relatively easy to talk about family intervention, the challenge is to identify appropriate support and mechanisms for its delivery. Dads in the interview sample demonstrated their belief in 'innate' fathering; something that cannot be learnt or changed. If their views represent those of other dads, it is unlikely that many fathers would see either the need or the value of parent support. Moreover, from the limited evidence that is available, it appears that few couples seek professional help for relationship difficulties such as conflict.

Non-resident fathers

Involvement

Recent research suggests that a lack of father involvement in the early post-divorce years is associated with a deteriorating father–child relationship over time (Ahrons and Tanner, 2003). So early involvement is crucial for continuing relationships. Non-resident fathers were rated as less involved than resident fathers (see Chapter Four). This is not surprising given their absence and the challenges of maintaining contact and involvement following divorce. This sample showed relatively high levels of contact compared with other research, probably because children who were in contact with their fathers would have been more inclined to complete a questionnaire about their father's involvement.

The insight into resident fathers' involvement permitted by the interviews points to the obstacles non-resident dads face in being a part of their children's lives. A large part of the 'being there' role of resident dads is not available to them, and they are tasked with establishing new roles and relationships if their contact is to be rewarding and effective. For example, because resident dads tend to be removed from 'hands-on' aspects of care, non-resident dads may benefit from help in arranging contact visits and ensuring the time they spend with children has a sense of normality and familiarity.

The interviews (see Chapter Three) show that children and parents see part of a father's role as providing. However, non-resident dads had lower ratings on their 'providing' role than resident fathers (see Chapter Four). Providing can be difficult when fathers remarry and must share their income between their old and new family and children may also perceive their father as providing less because of the impact of the divorce on family income. However, it is important to overcome these difficulties, as previous research has reported links between the payment of child support and children's well-being (Marsiglio and others, 2000; Harris, Furstenberg and Marmer, 1998).

Post-divorce parenting

The two factors associated with a fathers' post-separation involvement were mums' involvement and the relationship between the parents – findings in keeping with previous research (Coiro and Emery, 1998; Amato and Rezac, 1994). The research shows that the 'interrelatedness' of the family unit continues after separation or divorce. Recent longitudinal research has found this finding holds even into adulthood. Ahrons and Tanner (2003) found that how well parents get on in the first five years after their divorce can affect the father–child relationship for the next 20 years. Parents struggling with post-divorce conflict therefore require support in managing their differences so as to avoid long-term damage to the father–child relationship and the child's well-being.

Maintaining contact

An unexpected finding of the survey analysis was the lack of an association between children's well-being and non-resident dads' involvement. Possible biases in the sample (see Chapter Five) make it necessary to replicate this work with a more robust sample before conclusions can be drawn. However, if the finding holds, it could be explained by the evident difficulties non-resident fathers face in establishing a new role and way of relating to their children (see discussion above). The finding also has implications for policy on contact. The current emphasis on promoting contact needs to take account of the potentially detrimental impact on children of post-divorce conflict. Do the benefits of involvement outweigh the damage of parental conflict?

Directions for future research

The findings both echo those of previous research and provide new insight into what happens at home. The accounts of dads' involvement (Chapters Three and Six) reflect those of other in-depth work with families, in revealing dad's role as 'being there', providing and guiding (Warin and others, 1999). 'Jokey dads' are not a phenomenon confined to our sample, but have been found by others, such as Frosh, Phoenix and Pattman (2002) and Hatten, Vinter and Williams (2002). Previous research has also identified the importance of dads' ability to understand their children's lives and worlds (Amato, 1994) and get involved in activities with their children (Palkovitz, 1997). Yet both our work and that of others shows that fathers tend to be more a 'presence' in the home than someone actively managing their children's daily lives.

The research adds to the body of work seeking to understand what influences dads' involvement. In particular, the identification of more 'adult-centred' families provides insight into a group of families caught in a cycle of difficulties. Future research would be helpful in understanding more about why some families are vulnerable. Other considerations for future research are outlined below.

Getting a whole family perspective

The study sought to obtain the views of over 3,500 children and their parent figures. While the survey successfully obtained the views of large numbers of children or parents, it was less successful in obtaining the views of both parent figures and the child. It was especially difficult to get non-resident fathers to complete a questionnaire. The in-depth interviews reveal the value of recording a 'whole' family perspective, but the recruitment difficulties of the survey also reveal the challenge in doing this on a large scale and in a way that ensures the participation of a range of different types of families. Researchers interested in pursuing a whole family perspective will have to consider alternative recruitment processes if they are to obtain a more representative sample.

Understanding more about involvement and well-being

The regression analyses examining the factors associated with father involvement and with children's well-being provided helpful insight into the nature of these relationships. However, the models identified only a relatively small proportion of the factors that explain these relationships. For example, the model investigating non-resident dad's involvement explained 19 per cent of the variance in involvement. Further research is required to develop a fuller understanding of the questions in this study.

What determines children's well-being in separated families?

Unexpectedly, we found no link between non-resident fathers' involvement and their children's adjustment. This may be a result particular to this sample or it may be a genuine finding. Other researchers have reported similar results (Thomas and Forehand, 1993; Zill, 1988; Furstenberg, Morgan and Allison, 1987; Kurdek, 1986). Further research, building on this work with different samples of separated families is required before firm conclusions can be reached.

What mechanisms explain the associations?

The in-depth interviews complemented the survey in providing a greater understanding of how, for example, fathers' involvement was connected to mothers' involvement. However, questions remain about the mechanisms underlying the associations identified in the research. For example, why are fathers' gender attitudes important (see Chapter Six)? Do egalitarian gender attitudes directly influence dads' involvement because they reflect a belief that childcare is both 'his and her' work? Or do attitudes indirectly influence involvement because of their impact on the couple relationship? How does a mother's experience of her father's involvement affect her own? Do difficult children 'repel' their fathers' involvement or does a lack of a father's involvement lead to adjustment difficulties for the child?

Appendix A
Details of the number of questionnaires returned

Table A.1 Survey returns by school

Questionnaires	Inner city school	Suburban school	Rural school	Totals
Number of questionnaires distributed	1300	1300	900	3500
Number of families that opted out	20	40	39	99
Number of questionnaires returned: children (total legible returns)	1000	1000	800	2800 (2218)
parents	246	428	384	1058

Table A.2 The number of survey returns from different categories of respondent

Category of return	Number of returns from different categories of survey respondent	Returns within category	Proportion of returns within categories % (n)
Children's returns			
Total number of children	2218	Proportion of children with resident biological dad	69% (1517)
Total number of children with information on father	2198*	Proportion of children with 'social father'	2% (51)
		Proportion of children with non-resident dad	24% (520)
		Proportion of children with no father figure	5% (110)
Parent's returns			
Total number of parents	1091**		
Total number mothers	635	Proportion of resident fathers	92% (418***)
Total number fathers	452	Proportion of non-resident fathers	8% (34)
Couple and family returns			
Total number of couples	312	Proportion of intact families	88% (233)
Total number of families	265	Proportion of intact and biologically related families	77% (203)

*   20 children had missing data on presence of father-figure or relationship to father-figure.
**   Four parents did not state their gender.
*** 409 were used in the final analysis as for nine cases the data were incomplete.

Appendix B
Details of the scales used in the survey

Table B.1 Details of the scales used in the survey

Scale Details	Mothers (means, SD, and Cronbach's alphas)	Fathers (means, SD, and Cronbach's alphas)	Children (means, SD, and Cronbach's alphas)
Inventory of Parental Involvement (Hawkins and others, 2002) 26-item 5-point scale ranging from 26–130	111.2 (SD 12) Cronbach's alpha 0.85	103.7 (SD 15.6) Cronbach's alpha 0.91	Mark your father 104.7 (SD 23.7) Cronbach's alpha 0.97 Mark your mother Mean 114 (SD 16.6) Cronbach's alpha 0.95
Parenting Stress Scale (Abidin and Brunner, 1995) short form 20-item 5-point scale ranging from 20–100	36.2 (SD 15.2) Cronbach's alpha 0.94	37.2 (SD 14.8) Cronbach's alpha 0.94	
Strengths and Difficulties Questionnaire (Goodman, 1997) 25-item, 3-point scale ranging from 25–75	36.2 (SD 7.2) Cronbach's alpha 0.86	36.2 (SD 7.2) Cronbach's alpha 0.86	40.7 (SD 6.5) Cronbach's alpha 0.77
General Health Questionnaire 12 (Goldberg, 1978; Goldberg and Williams 1988) 12-item, 4-point scale ranging from 12–48	23.7 (SD 5.7) Cronbach's alpha 0.90	23.6 (SD 5.7) Cronbach's alpha 0.91	
Self-esteem Scale shortened (Rosenberg, 1965) 7-item, 5-point scale ranging from 7–35	28.9 (SD 5.6) Cronbach's alpha 0.87	29.3 (SD 5.4) Cronbach's alpha 0.88	26.7 (SD 5.6) Cronbach's alpha 0.81
Gender Equality Scale (Wiggins and Bynner, 1993) 8-item 5-point scale ranging from 8–40	31.9 (SD 4.8) Cronbach's alpha 0.71	30 (SD 5.8) Cronbach's alpha 0.81	

Modified Parenting Inventory (Abidin and Brunner, 1995) 9-item 5-point scale ranging from 9–45	16.4 (SD 7.3) Cronbach's alpha 0.86	15.6 (SD 6.1) Cronbach's alpha 0.80	
Own Father Involvement (from NCDS) 5-item 5-point scale ranging from 5–25	15. (SD 5.6) Cronbach's alpha 0.88	13.8 (SD 5.1) Cronbach's alpha 0.88	
Own Mother Involvement (from NCDS) 4-item 5-point scale ranging from 4–20	14.6 (SD 3.8) Cronbach's alpha 0 .83	13.6 (SD 3.9) Cronbach's alpha 0 .84	
Conflict Scale shortened (Grych, Seid and Fincham, 1992) 9-item scale ranging from 9–37			12.9 (SD 4.1) Cronbach's alpha 0.85

Appendix C
The Inventory of Father Involvement

Figure C.1 Sample questions from the Inventory of Father Involvement

WHAT DO YOUR PARENTS DO WITH YOU?

1. What mark would you give dad for the job he is doing in bringing you up?

		very good	good	average	poor	very poor
1.	Disciplining you	☐	☐	☐	☐	☐
2.	Encouraging you to help at home	☐	☐	☐	☐	☐
4.	Encouraging you to succeed in school	☐	☐	☐	☐	☐
10.	Providing your basic needs (e.g. food, clothing)	☐	☐	☐	☐	☐
13.	Spending time talking with you when you want to talk about something	☐	☐	☐	☐	☐
16.	Praising you for something you have done well	☐	☐	☐	☐	☐
20.	Planning for your future (e.g. education, training)	☐	☐	☐	☐	☐
23.	Helping you with your homework	☐	☐	☐	☐	☐
24.	Attending events you take part in (e.g. sports, school events)	☐	☐	☐	☐	☐
25.	Taking care of your basic needs/activities (e.g. taking you to places)	☐	☐	☐	☐	☐
26.	Knowing where you go and what you do with your friends	☐	☐	☐	☐	☐

Figure C.2 The nine dimensions of fathering on the Inventory of Father Involvement (Hawkins and others, 2002)

Discipline and teaching responsibility
Disciplining your children
Encouraging your children to do their chores
Setting rules and limits for your children's behaviour

School encouragement
Encouraging your children to succeed in school
Encouraging your children to do their homework
Teaching your children to follow rules at school

Mother support
Giving your children's mother encouragement and emotional support
Letting your children know that their mother is an important and special person
Cooperating with your children's mother in the rearing of your children

Providing
Providing your children's basic needs (food, clothing, shelter and health care)
Accepting responsibility for the financial support of the children you have fathered

Time and talking together
Being a pal or a friend to your children
Spending time just talking with your children when they want to talk about something
Spending time with your children doing things they like to do

Praise and affection
Praising your children for being good or doing the right thing
Praising your children for something they have done well
Telling your children that you love them

Developing talents and future concerns
Encouraging your children to develop their talents
Encouraging your children to continue their schooling beyond high school
Planning for your children's future (education, training)

Reading and homework support
Encouraging your children to read
Reading to your younger children
Helping your older children with their homework

Attentiveness
Attending events your children participate in (sports, school, church events)
Being involved in the daily or regular routine of taking care of your children's basic needs or activities (feeding, driving them places, etc.)
Knowing where your children go and what they do with their friends

Appendix D
The interview sample

Table D.1 The selection process

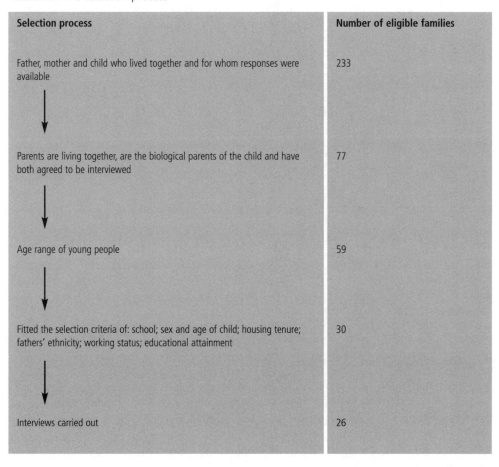

Selection process	Number of eligible families
Father, mother and child who lived together and for whom responses were available	233
Parents are living together, are the biological parents of the child and have both agreed to be interviewed	77
Age range of young people	59
Fitted the selection criteria of: school; sex and age of child; housing tenure; fathers' ethnicity; working status; educational attainment	30
Interviews carried out	26

Table D.2 The interview sample compared to the family sample

Characteristics	The family sample from the survey n=233 (%)	The interview sample n=26
Qualifications (of fathers):		
None	23 (18%)	4
CSE/O Level/GCSE	52 (40%)	11
A Level	15 (12%)	3
University	40 (31%)	8
Employment (of fathers):		
Full-time	208 (84%)	23
Part-time	22 (9%)	2
Not in paid work	17 (7%)	1
Employment (of mothers):		
Full-time	120 (47%)	14
Part-time	94 (37%)	10
Not in paid work	39 (15%)	2
Housing tenure:		
Owner-occupied	207 (80%)	20
LA/Council	42 (16%)	5
Other	11 (4%)	1
Ethnicity (of fathers):		
White British	190 (73%)	20
White Irish	4 (2%)	2
Other White	9 (4%)	1
Indian	22 (9%)	2
Other Asian	5 (2%)	1
Parental age range:		
Father	29-68	35-58
Mother	29-60	30-54
Young people's age range:		
Male	11-17	12-16
Female	11-17	11-16
Young people's sex:		
Male	152 (58%)	15
Female	112 (42%)	11
School group:		
Rural	95 (36%)	10
Suburban	109 (41%)	9
Inner city	95 (22%)	7

Appendix E
Mean scores for ratings of different dimensions of father-figures' involvement

Table E.1 Means scores for ratings on different dimensions of father figures' involvement

	Resident fathers		Non-resident fathers	
	Mean score	Standard deviation	Mean score	Standard deviation
Discipline**	12.24	2.38	10.66	3.52
School encouragement**	12.82	2.41	11.59	3.4
Mother support**	13.06	2.45	10.64	3.87
Providing+**	9.14	1.38	7.96	2.49
Talking together*	12	3.01	11.49	3.52
Praise**	12.71	2.7	12.09	3.28
Developing talents**	12.83	2.44	11.50	3.28
Reading and homework support**	11.8	2.97	10.38	3.73
Attentiveness**	12.29	2.68	10.8	3.57

+   Maximum possible score of 10, all other dimensions scored to 15.
*   p<0.01
** p<0.001.

Appendix F
Variables included in the regression models

Table F.1 Variables included in the regression models

	Child's well-being and resident dad involvement	Child's well-being and non-resident dad involvement	Factors predicting resident dad's involvement (dads' accounts)	Factors predicting non-resident dad's contact	Factors predicting non-resident dad's involvement
Family factors					
Interparental conflict					
Father report	x		x		
Mother report					
Child report		x		x	x
Child receives free school meals	x	x	x	x	x
Number of siblings	x		x		
Infrequent contact with father (separated families)		x			
Time since separation (non-intact families)		x		x	x
Father factors					
Level of involvement					
Father's measure	x		x		
Child's measure		x		x	x
Own father's involvement			x		
Own mother's involvement			x		
Gender equality attitudes			x		
Self-esteem/mental health	x		x		
General health			x		
Employment			x		
Educational achievement	x		x		

Age			x		
Father living with new partner		x		x	x
Biological/social father	x				
Mother factors					
Level of involvement					
Mother's measure			x		
Child's measure		x		x	x
Own father's involvement			x		
Own mother's involvement			x		
Gender equality attitudes			x		
Self-esteem			x		
General health			x		
Employed full or part-time			x		
Educational attainment			x		
Age			x		
Mother living with new partner		x		x	x
Child factors					
Age	x	x	x	x	x
Emotional and behavioural problems	x		x		
Father report					
Mother report		x			
Child report					
Gender	x	x	x	x	x

Appendix G
Details of the regression models

Table G.1 Factors (standardised beta coefficients) predicting child-reported emotional and behavioural problems (resident fathers' sample)

Child receives free school meals	0.032
High levels of education in father*	-0.111
Large family size	-0.011
Older child	0.012
Female child**	-0.138
Mental health problems in father*	0.131
High levels of interparental conflict***	0.176
Biological father*	-0.132
High levels of father involvement***	-0.246

*p<.05; **p<.01; ***p<.001.

The regression model was significant ($F_{(9,255)}=7.528$, $p<.001$), and explained 18 per cent of the variance in children's emotional and behavioural well-being

Table G.2 Factors (standardised beta coefficients) predicting child-reported emotional and behavioural problems (non-resident fathers' sample)

Child receives free school meals	0.047
Time since parents separated+	0.149
Father lives with another partner	0.043
Mother lives with another partner	-0.112
Female child	-0.074
Child's age	-0.026
High levels of interparental conflict (child's report)***	0.356
Higher levels of mother involvement**	-0.25
Father's low frequency of visitation	0.113
Higher levels of father involvement	0.06

+p<.10; **p<.01; ***p<.001.

The regression model was significant ($F_{(10,139)}=4.47$, $p<.001$) and explained 19 per cent of the variance in non-resident fathers' children's emotional and behavioural well-being.

Table G.3 Factors (standardised beta coefficients) predicting father-reported father involvement

Child receives free school meals	0.02
Number of siblings	-0.08
Female child	-0.05
Child's age	-0.09
Child's emotional/behavioural problems (father's report)*	-0.17
Father's age	-0.1
Father's educational attainment	-0.01
Father is employed (full- or part-time)	-0.11
Father's General Health Questionnaire score	-0.04
Father's self-esteem+	0.2
Father's gender equality attitudes**	0.22
Father's own mother's involvement	-0.01
Father's own father's involvement	0.13
Mother's age	0.15
Mother's educational attainment	-0.06
Mother is employed full-time	-0.09
Mother is employed part-time+	-0.27
Mother's General Health Questionnaire score	-0.03
Mother's self-esteem	-0.06
Mother's gender equality attitudes	-0.04
Mother's own mother's involvement	-0.04
Mother's own father's involvement	0.06
Mother's involvement**	0.28
High levels of interparental conflict (father's report)	-0.13

+$p<.10$; *$p<.05$; **$p<.01$.

The overall regression model was significant ($F_{(24,94)}=3.65$, $p<.001$). In all, 35 per cent of the variance in self-reported father involvement was explained by the variables in the model.

Table G.4 Factors (standardised beta coefficients) predicting child-reported non-resident father's contact (the matched families' sample)

Child receives free school meals	-0.018
Time since parents separated***	0.246
Father lives with another partner	-0.094
Mother lives with another partner	-0.052
Female child	0.035
Child's age	0.058
High levels of interparental conflict (child's report)+	0.11

+p<.10; ***p<.001.

The model was significant (F(7,270)=3.72, p<.001), but managed to explain only 6 per cent of the variance in non-resident fathers' frequency of contact with their children.

Table G.5 Factors (standardised beta coefficients) predicting child-reported non-resident father's involvement

Free school meals	-0.001
Time since parents separated+	-0.119
Father lives with another partner	0.06
Mother lives with another partner	-0.019
Female child	-0.042
Child's age	-0.123
Higher levels of mother's involvement*** (child's report)	0.374
High levels of interparental conflict (child's report)**	-0.187

+p<.10; **p<.01; ***p<.001

The overall regression model was significant (F(8,183)=6.61, p<.001). The amount of variance in non-resident fathers' involvement explained by the factors in the model was 19 per cent.

References

Abidin, R R and Brunner, J F (1995) 'Development of a Parenting Alliance Inventory', *Journal of Clinical Child Psychology*, 24, 31–40

Ahrons, C and Tanner, J (2003) 'Adult children and their fathers: relationship changes 20 years after parental divorce', *Family Relations*, 52, 340–51

Amato, P R (1994) 'Father–child relations, mother–child relations, and offspring psychological well-being in early adulthood', *Journal of Marriage and the Family*, 56, 1031–42

Amato, P R and Gilbreth, J G (1999) 'Non-resident fathers and children's well-being: a meta-analysis', *Journal of Marriage and the Family*, 61, 557–74

Amato, P R and Keith, B (1991) 'Parental divorce and the well-being of children: a meta-analysis', *Psychological Bulletin*, 110, 26–46

Amato, P R and Rezac, S (1994) 'Contact with non-resident parents, interparental conflict, and children's behaviour', *Journal of Family Issues*, 15, 191–207

Buchanan, A, Katz, A and McCoy, A (1999) *Leading Lads*. Young Voice

Cabrera, N J, Tamis-LeMonda, S, Bradley, R H, Hofferth, S and Lamb, M E (2000) 'Fatherhood in the twenty-first century', *Child Development*, 71, 127–36

Carlson, M J and McLanahan, S S (2001) 'Fragile families, father involvement, and public policy'. *Working Paper 01-24-FF*. Center for Research on Child Wellbeing

Coiro, M J and Emery, R E (1998) 'Do marriage problems affect fathering more than mothering? A quantitative and qualitative review', *Clinical Child and Family Psychology Review*, 1, 23–40

Coltrane, S (1996) *Family man*. New York: Oxford University Press

Crockett, L J, Eggebeen, D J and Hawkins, A J (1993) 'Father's presence and young children's behavioral and cognitive adjustment', *Family Relations*, 14, 355–77

Doherty, W J, Kouneski, E F and Erickson, M F (1998) 'Responsible fathering: an overview and conceptual framework', *Journal of Marriage and the Family*, 60, 277–92

Eggebeen, D J and Knoester, C (2001) 'Does fatherhood matter for men?', *Journal of Marriage and Family*, 63, May, 381–93

Feldman, R (2000) 'Parents' convergence on sharing and marital satisfaction, father involvement, and parent–child relationship at the transition to parenthood', *Infant Mental Health Journal*, 21, 176–91

Flouri, E and Buchanan, A (2003) 'The role of father involvement in children's later mental health', *Journal of Adolescence*, 26, 63–78

Flouri, E and Buchanan, A (2003) 'What predicts fathers' involvement with their children? A prospective study of intact families', *British Journal of Developmental Psychology*, 21, 81–97

Frosh, S, Phoenix, A and Pattman, R (2002) *Young Masculinities: Understanding Boys in Contemporary Society*. Palgrave

Furstenberg, F, Morgan, S P and Allison, P D (1987) 'Paternal participation and children's well-being after marital dissolution', *American Sociological Review*, 52, 5, 695–701

Furstenberg, F F Jr and Nord, C W (1985) 'Parenting Apart: Patterns of Childrearing After Marital Disruption', *Journal of Marriage and the Family*, 47, 893–904

Gerson, K (1993) *No Man's Land. Men's Changing Commitments to Family and Work*. New York: Basic Books

Goldberg, D P (1978) *Manual of the General Health Questionnaire*. NFER-Nelson

Goldberg, D P and Williams, P (1988) *A user's guide to the General Health Questionnaire*. NFER-Nelson

Goodman, R (1997) 'The Strengths and Difficulties Questionnaire: a research note', *Journal of Child Psychology and Psychiatry*, 38, 581–6

Grolnick, W S, Benjet, C, Kurowski, C O and Apostoleris, N H (1997) 'Predictors of parent involvement in children's schooling', *Journal of Educational Psychology*, 89, 538–48

Grych, J H and Fincham, F D (1999) 'The adjustment of children from divorced families: implications of empirical research for clinical intervention' *in* Galatzer-Levy, R M and Kraus, L *eds The scientific basis of child custody decisions*. New York: John Wiley and Sons Inc

Grych, J H, Seid, M and Fincham, F D (1992) 'Assessing marital conflict from the child's perspective', *Child Development*, 63, 558–72

Harris, K, Furstenberg, F and Marmer, J K (1998) 'Paternal involvement with adolescents in intact families: the influence of fathers over the life course', *Demography*, 35, 2, 201–16

Hatten, W, Vinter, L and Williams, R (2002) *Dads on Dads: Needs and expectations at home and at work.* Equal Opportunities Commission

Hawkins, A J, Bradford, K P, Palkovitz, R, Christiansent, S L, Day, R D and Call, V R A (2002) 'The inventory of father involvement: a pilot study of a new measure of father involvement', *Journal of Men's Studies*, 10, 183–96

Hetherington, E M and Stanley-Hagan, M M (1997) 'The effects of divorce on fathers and their children' *in* Lamb, M E *ed. The Role of the Father in Child Development*, pp. 191–210. New York: Wiley

Hetherington, E M and Stanley-Hagan, M (1999) 'The adjustment of children with divorced parents: a risk and resiliency perspective', *Journal of Child Psychology and Psychiatry*, 140, 1, 129–40

Hofferth, S L and Anderson, K G (2003) 'Are all Dads equal? Biology versus marriage as a basis for paternal investment', *Journal of Marriage and Family*, 65, 213–32

Katz, A, Buchanan, A and Ten Brinke, J (1997) *The Can-Do Girls.* Young Voice

King, V (1994) 'Non-resident father involvement and child well-being. Can dads make a difference?', *Journal of Family Issues*, 15, 1, 78–96

Kurdek, L A (1986) 'Custodial mothers' perceptions of visitation and payment of child support by non-custodial fathers in families with low and high levels of pre-separation interparent conflict', *Journal of Applied-Developmental Psychology*, 7, 4, 307–23

Lamb, M E (1986) 'The changing role of fathers' *in* Lamb, M E *ed. The Father's Role: Applied Perspectives.* New York: John Wiley

Lamb, M E *ed.* (1997) *The role of the father in child development.* New York: John Wiley

Lewis, C (2000) *A Man's Place in the Home: Fathers and Families in the UK.* Joseph Rowntree Foundation

Lewis, C, Maka, Z and Papacosta, A (1997) 'Why do fathers become disengaged from their children's lives? Maternal and paternal accounts of divorce in Greece', *Journal of Divorce and Remarriage*, 28, 89–117

Lord Chancellor's Department (LCD) (2002) *Making Contact Work: A report to the Lord Chancellor on the facilitation of arrangements for contact between children and their non-residential parents and the enforcement of court orders for contact.* LCD

Lupton, D and Barclay, L (1997) *Constructing Fatherhood: Discourses and Experiences.* Sage

Maclean, M and Eekelaar, J (1997) *The parental obligation: A study of parenthood across households.* Hart

Marsiglio, W, Amato, P, Day, R D and Lamb, M E (2000) 'Scholarship on fatherhood in the 1990s and beyond', *Journal of Marriage and the Family*, 62, November, 1173–91

McBride, B A and Rane, T R (1998) 'Parenting Alliance as a predictor of father involvement: an exploratory study', *Family Relations*, 47, 229–36

McBride, B A, Rane, T R, Schoppe, S J and Ho, M (in press) 'Multiple determinants of father involvement: an exploratory study using the PSID-CDS data set' *in* Day, R and Lamb, M E *eds Measuring father involvement.* Mahwah, NJ: Erlbaum

Palkovitz, R (1997) 'Reconstructing "involvement". Expanding conceptualizations of men's caring in contemporary families' *in* Hawkins, A J and Dollahite, D C *Generative Fathering*, pp. 200–16. Sage

Pleck, J H (1997) 'Paternal involvement: levels, sources, and consequences' *in* Lamb, M E *ed. The Role of the Father in Child Development*, pp. 66–103. New York: Wiley

Pleck, E H and Pleck, J H (1997) 'Fatherhood ideals in the United States: historical dimensions' *in* Lamb, M E *ed. The Role of the Father in Child Development.* New York: Wiley

Reynolds, J *ed.* (2001) *Not in front of the children? How conflict between parents affects children.* One Plus One

Roberts, G C, Block, J H and Block, J (1984) 'Continuity and change in parents' child-rearing practices', *Child Development*, 55, 586–97

Rogers, B and Pryor, J (1998) *Divorce and separation. The outcomes for children.* Joseph Rowntree Foundation

Rosenberg, M (1965) *Society and the adolescent self-image.* Princeton: Princeton University Press

Thomas, A M and Forehand, R (1993) 'The role of paternal variables in divorced and married families: predictability of adolescent adjustment', *American Journal of Orthopsychiatry*, 63, 1, 126–35

Trinder, L, Beek, M and Connolly, J (2002) *Making Contact Work. How parents and children negotiate and experience contact after divorce.* JRF: York Publishing Services

van Bakel, H J and Riksen-Walraven, J M (2002) 'Parenting and development of one-year olds: links with parental, contextual, and child characteristics', *Child Development*, 73, 256–73

Volling, B L and Belsky, J (1991) 'Multiple determinants of father involvement during infancy in dual-earner and single-earner families', *Journal of Marriage and the Family*, 53, 461–74

Warin, J, Solomon, Y, Lewis, C and Langford, W (1999) *Fathers, Work and Family Life.* Family Policy Studies Centre

Wiggins, R D and Bynner, J (1993) 'Social attitudes' *in* Ferri, E *ed Life at 33: The Fifth follow-up of the National Child Development Study.* National Children's Bureau

Zill, N (1988) 'Behavior, achievement, and health problems among children in stepfamilies: findings from a national survey of child health' *in* Hetherington, E M and Arasteh, J D *eds Impact of divorce, single parenting, and stepparenting on children*, pp. 325–68. Hillsdale, NJ, and England: Lawrence Erlbaum Associates